P

ALA

Shaun Campbell is a s... is a regular contributor to the football magazine *FourFourTwo* and *African Soccer*. This is his first book.

Alan Shearer

Shaun Campbell

PUFFIN BOOKS

PUFFIN BOOKS

Published by the Penguin Group
Penguin Books Ltd, 27 Wrights Lane, London w8 5tz, England
Penguin Books USA Inc., 375 Hudson Street, New York, New York 10014, USA
Penguin Books Australia Ltd, Ringwood, Victoria, Australia
Penguin Books Canada Ltd, 10 Alcorn Avenue, Toronto, Ontario, Canada m4v 3b2
Penguin Books (NZ) Ltd, 182–190 Wairau Road, Auckland 10, New Zealand

Penguin Books Ltd, Registered Offices: Harmondsworth, Middlesex, England

First published 1997
3 5 7 9 10 8 6 4 2

Set in Monotype Baskerville
Typeset by Rowland Phototypesetting Ltd,
Bury St Edmunds, Suffolk
Made and printed in England by Clays Ltd, St Ives plc

British Library Cataloguing in Publication Data
A CIP catalogue record for this book is available from the British Library

isbn 0–140–38638–6

Contents

CHAPTER ONE

Coming Home

M ONDAY, 29 JULY 1996. The news was simply too big, too important, to be kept secret. Hours before any official announcement had been made the word passed round the football-crazy city of Newcastle like wildfire. *Alan Shearer had signed.* Alan Shearer was coming home.

Many refused to believe it. After all, only a couple of weeks earlier the newspapers had been full of stories about him going to Manchester United. Before that there had been much talk of him leaving England for Italy, probably to play for AC Milan. As for the man himself, all he had ever said on the subject was that he was perfectly happy at Blackburn Rovers.

But then, at 10.30 a.m., the rumour was finally confirmed. All over Britain TV and radio stations interrupted their programmes with a newsflash. 'Alan

Shearer, England's centre-forward, has completed a £15-million move to Newcastle United.'

By lunch-time the streets to St James' Park, Newcastle's ground, were full of people. The club was practically empty, because the staff and players were actually on a pre-season friendly tour of the Far East. Even so, St James still drew the crowds like a magnet. Workers took an extended lunch-break to make a pilgrimage to this football shrine. Children joined them in a dancing and singing line through the streets of Newcastle. The first day of their summer holidays had started better than anyone had dared hope. Soon a queue formed outside the club shop as the fans lined up to buy shirts with the name of their hero above the number nine on the famous black-and-white striped kit.

The press conference at St James' Park the following Monday drew a crowd almost as big as a Premiership match's. More than 12,000 excited supporters ignored the pouring rain as they stood outside the ground, listening to the reporters' questions and Alan's answers relayed on the public-address system. The biggest cheer came when Alan was asked if this was his last move. 'I hope so,' he said, before adding with typical modesty, 'Who knows? If I don't score for twelve games they may kick me out.' Nobody believed for a second that this would ever happen.

The Newcastle fans were getting used to the thrill of big-money signings. In 1995 alone nearly £20 million had been spent on Les Ferdinand, Faustino Asprilla, David Ginola and David Batty. But you had to go back 14 years, to 1982, to find an occasion that matched the excitement of that July day. Nobody remembered it better than Alan. At the age of 12 he had queued outside St James' Park for six hours to watch Kevin Keegan make his debut for the club. He shouted himself hoarse when Keegan scored with a diving header. As a player Keegan had been Alan's hero, the man whose skills and enthusiasm had done most to inspire him. Obviously Keegan the manager thought as highly of Alan. Why else would he be prepared to pay a world-record transfer fee of £15 million to get his man?

The Newcastle fans were sure Keegan had made the right decision, even though the club already had an attacking line-up of hugely expensive star players. They knew that in Alan they were getting something extra special. This was the man who had scored a hat trick on his first full league appearance at the age of only 17. Here was the only player since the 1930s to have scored more than 30 goals 3 seasons running. Here also was the man who had just emerged from Euro 96 as Europe's deadliest striker. And to cap it all here was a local boy, a Geordie through and through.

Alan Shearer was coming home.

CHAPTER TWO

Jack, the Scout

H E STOOD APART from the little groups of spectators on the muddy touch-line. His hands were pushed deep into his pockets and his cap pulled down against the cold. He was old enough to be the grandfather of any of the 12- and 13-year-old Newcastle schoolboys on the pitch. But Jack Hixon was neither family nor friend to any of them. He was a scout – one of those unpaid and unrecognized heroes of the game who travel all over Britain in search of new young talent for the professional clubs.

What caught Hixon's eye was the blond youngster playing up front for the Newcastle City team. He was smaller and lighter than many of the other lads, and when he tried to shield the ball he often got bumped off it by one of the beefier opposition defenders. He didn't have much of a left foot, either. But Hixon saw beyond that. He recognized, almost instantly, the qualities that would one day make this boy a successful professional. It wasn't simply his good sense of position, his ability to be in the right place at the right time. Nor was it the lad's obvious enthusiasm. What made him stand out to Hixon was his will to *win*.

A few weeks later Hixon watched him play again, this time for the Wallsend Boys' Club. Now he was sure. When the game was over he approached the lad's father and asked him if his son would be interested in a trial for Southampton. 'Ask him yourself, he's old enough to make up his own mind,' was the reply. In fact, Mr Shearer had no doubt what his son's answer would be. A trial, especially for a first-division club, was the first rung on the ladder that young Alan had been dreaming of climbing for years.

Alan Shearer was born on 13 August 1970 in Gosforth, Newcastle, bang in the middle of one of the great football centres of the world. The north-east of England has produced some of the finest players, and the most loyal supporters, since the very beginnings of the game. Alan now reckons he had little choice in his career. 'As soon as you could walk they would throw a ball at your feet and say, "Go on, kick it,"' is how he remembers his earliest days with older sister Karen and his parents, Alan and Anne. His father,

6

a sheet-metal worker, was a great football fan and Newcastle United supporter. By the time Alan was five years old he was posing for photographs in the back garden in his first Newcastle strip. And every spare minute was spent playing football.

Anywhere and anything would do. If he wasn't kicking a ball around with his dad in the garden, he was playing with the other boys in the yards of the council estate, or on the wasteground near by. The goal could be a pair of garage doors or a couple of jackets slung on the ground. The ball was sometimes no more than a tin can. The main attraction of school was the chance to play organized games.

Of course, Alan wasn't the only young Geordie obsessed with football. What made him unusual, though, was his total commitment. To say that he was serious about football makes it sound as though it wasn't fun. It was, but for Alan it was more than that. He enjoyed it so much that he was determined to make football his life.

Inevitably this caused trouble at school. He wasn't a difficult boy, just one who had his mind on one thing only. Although this exasperated his teachers, they couldn't help admiring his single-mindedness. On one occasion Alan wrote down 'dustman' on a careers advice form, a joke for which his dad gave him a clout and told him to put down 'joiner'. Both of them knew better. When it came to meeting the careers officer Alan bluntly told him that he was going to be a professional footballer. No question.

Looking back now Alan recognizes that he should have tried harder at other things, just in case he didn't make it. But he was so sure that he would succeed in football that he couldn't be bothered. He was once awarded grade one in an oral English exam. Hardly surprising when you learn that the subject he talked about was football . . .

Whatever else you could say about his school record, you have to admit that he was good at football. By the time he was 8 he was playing with the 9- and 10-year-olds in the school team. And scoring goals. He had always got a special buzz out of scoring, whether it was playing one-on-one with a mate in a street on the estate, or on the school playing-fields with a proper goal and a net. Somewhere along the line, in those quickfire backstreet games, Alan found the knack of scoring goals, the key to the style that would later make him one of the most sought-after players in the world.

His early successes fuelled his enthusiasm and determination. Alan still remembers the thrill of learning that he had been given the school team's captaincy rather than a rival boy, Andrew McTaggart. He didn't always get to play up front, though.

There were times when his keenness and his insistence on being involved in everything from goal-kicks to penalties resulted in him being placed in the heart of the midfield.

Nothing set Alan back, not even his first injury. An awkward tackle in a school match rammed the bottom of his shin-pad into his leg, leaving a cut that needed six stitches. It hurt, but the pain was lessened by the feeling of being just like a real professional player as he spent the next few days hobbling around on crutches.

When Alan moved up to secondary school he moved up the footballing ladder, playing for the city in six- and seven-a-side football, and then for Northumberland in county competitions. He made an impact wherever he went, though more because of his personality and enthusiasm than his footballing ability. The city and county matches were generally friendlies, where it was more important to develop skills and enjoy the game than to win. They provided some marvellous opportunities for the young foot-ballers, with tournaments sometimes being held on the hallowed turf of St James' Park. But Alan still wanted more.

One of his teachers suggested he got in touch with one of the many boys' clubs in the north-east. They played their matches on Sundays, which would allow

Alan to fill his whole weekend with football. He went along to the Wallsend Boys' Club, where Peter Beardsley and Steve Bruce had started out, and asked first if he could just train with them. The club's manager, Sid Sharpe, was hugely impressed by the boy's maturity and straightforward manner. Most kids got their parents to introduce them to the club, but Alan was prepared to make his own way in the world. He was only 12, but already he knew the difference between dreaming about being a professional player and taking the steps to make it happen.

This part of Alan's character had come from his parents. Although they were never well off, they supported his dream. Somehow they found the money for new kit and boots, and turned up in all weathers to cheer him on from the touch-line.

Money was tight but Alan found ways of making football pay. He would play one-on-one in the street with his mate Gary Hayes for 10p a goal. More often than not Gary would end up with his £2-a-week pocket money jingling in Alan's pocket. On one occasion Wallsend were winning 13–0, but Alan hadn't scored. He'd hit the post, hit the bar, everything but get a goal. His dad, on the touch-line as usual, shouted out that he'd bet a pound Alan wouldn't score. It was a bad move. In the next five minutes Alan got three touches – and three goals.

He'd been going with his dad to watch Newcastle for a few years by then. But there was a special reason for going at the start of the 1982/83 season, even though they weren't in the top division. Kevin Keegan had shocked the football world by his decision to leave Southampton and join Newcastle. Such was the popularity of the little curly-haired forward that the gates practically doubled overnight. After queuing for six hours, Alan watched Keegan make his first appearance in the black-and-white strip, against Queens Park Rangers. He scored. Newcastle won and Alan had found his first role model.

Keegan wasn't born a great player, unlike Pelé or Johan Cruyff. He made himself one. Nobody worked harder than Keegan to improve his game, or gave more of himself on the pitch. He was also a *quick* player, sharp and dangerous in the penalty area, always looking to strike. Much the same would be said of Alan Shearer a few years later.

In his first season at Newcastle, Keegan scored 21 goals and Alan saw every one at St James' Park. He never missed a Keegan appearance at Newcastle in the two years he was there. Alan watched Keegan, studied him, then went home to practise what he had seen – the turns, the shots, the diving headers. There were other good players in the Newcastle team –

especially the two local boys just breaking through, Peter Beardsley and Chris Waddle – but it was Keegan who most inspired Alan. He actually came face to face with his idol one day. His mother entered him in a competition in the local newspaper to meet Keegan at the Newcastle training ground. Alan was one of the lucky winners. Nothing could have given him greater pleasure.

This was the lad Jack Hixon first saw in 1983. Slightly small for his age and a bit one-footed, but with an enthusiasm and a feeling for the game that more than made up for any weaknesses. Football crazy, but football serious. Like all good scouts of youngsters, Hixon knew that the key to spotting future talent lies in recognizing how much potential remains. To see the player not as he is now, but what he will become.

Alan was still a bit of a lightweight, but only because he was a late developer. As he grew and filled out, the knocks he had taken from the heavier lads, and the skills he had learned to avoid them, would prove vital. His all-round game would improve, provided he was prepared to work at it, something Hixon knew would not be a problem. And there was one thing about him that you couldn't underestimate. Somehow or other he always seemed to get in a shot or two – and a good number of them went in.

There was a strong north-east connection with Southampton in the early 1980s. The Saints' manager, Lawrie McMenemy, was a Geordie, so was the youth coach, Dave Merrington. And of course, there was Hixon himself. Perhaps all that flashed through Alan's mind in the split second before he said yes to Hixon's offer of a trial with the south-coast club 300 miles away from home.

Later, a myth grew up about Alan's decision to start his professional career with Southampton. It was said that Newcastle had played him in goal in a trial and so hadn't spotted his potential. It's not quite the whole truth.

Alan *did* have a trial at Newcastle, and he *did* play in goal, during some five-a-side games, but so did many of the others. Newcastle had a lot of lads on trial, but not many keepers, so several of the outfield players had volunteered to take a turn between the posts. It was typical of Alan that he should have been one of them.

Newcastle liked what they saw – when Alan was playing up front at least – and made their interest obvious. But Alan was growing closer and closer to Southampton. In Jack Hixon he had found someone he could trust without question. It wasn't just a matter of Jack being the first to recognize that burning desire to succeed, he knew the game from the inside and could give the advice young Alan so badly needed. Though something like 50 years apart in age, the two became friends. Even now, 14 years later, they remain in almost daily contact.

There were other aspects about Southampton that appealed to Alan. The thought that it might be easier to break into first-team football with a smaller club went through his mind. He also knew that if he was going to make it as a professional he would have to play outside his home town. Hadn't Kevin Keegan spent three years in Germany with Hamburg?

It wasn't a decision that Alan made overnight. He signed Associated Schoolboy forms with South-ampton a few weeks after his fourteenth birthday. At one stage in the trials he knew he was on the verge of being dropped, until he scored a crucial goal. That was the second rung of the ladder successfully climbed. He had nearly two more years to wait before he could go further and be accepted on the Youth Trainee Scheme (YTS).

Alan filled the time the only way he knew how – with football. He started playing for Cramlington Juniors, another boys' club, in his final school year and showed some cracking form. Once, against a team called Brass Tacks, he scored 13 goals in a 17-goal thrashing that the referee stopped with 10 minutes still remaining. At the end of the season, still only 15 years old, he played in the Cramlington Juniors Under-16 team that won an under-18 inter-county competition. In the final, with the scores locked in the last minute, Alan was fouled in the penalty area. He picked himself up, put the ball on the spot and fired it cleanly home.

It wasn't a bad way to say goodbye to the world of school and boys' club football, a world that had taught him much and which he looks back on today with great affection. But the time had come for the third step on the career ladder. At Easter 1986 Alan had undergone his final pre-YTS assessment for Southampton. In July, a month before his sixteenth birthday, he committed himself, signing with the club as a trainee. There wouldn't be much in the wage packet – just £25 a week – and he would be a long way from his family and friends. From now on, though, Alan would be doing what he had always wanted, making a career in professional football.

CHAPTER THREE

A Hat Trick for Starters

D AVE MERRINGTON WAS more than just the youth-team coach. To the 16- and 17-year-olds under his wing, he was their teacher, their boss and surrogate uncle all rolled into one. For Alan, in particular, there was something very comforting about Merrington's Geordie accent, even when it was bellowing instructions on the training field that were hard to follow. It was a constant reminder of his home in the north-east, which suddenly seemed a very long way away.

As the trainees settled into their new lives, they found that Merrington was always ready to listen to their problems. But they soon learned that he was anything but a soft touch. Alan well remembers one occasion when the coach overheard him arguing with a fellow trainee over whose turn it was to do a particular job. 'I'll show you whose turn it is, bonny lad,' Merrington said. 'Be at the ground at seven tomorrow morning, ready to start work.'

Another time, Alan left a tap running in the boot-room, where his job that day was to scrape the mud off the professional players' boots. The water overflowed the sink and flooded the medical room. Merrington made all the trainees run round the pitch 50 times for that mistake, a punishment that made Alan less than popular for a day or two.

What Merrington was trying to teach them was that football is a team game. If one player stuffs up, the whole team suffers. They had to take responsibility not just for themselves, but for each other. Like all lessons in football, it was one Alan learned quickly.

Alan was living in digs with Nigel and Maureen Wareham, who treated him, he says, like an adopted son. Their home was only five minutes' walk from the ground, which meant that he could keep the £10-a-week that the club gave him for a bus pass to add to the £25-a-week he earned from the YTS.

Alan was homesick for the first few months, but a couple of other lads from the north-east were in the youth team squad, which helped. One of them, Neil Maddison, lived just around the corner. They spent their spare time going to the cinema, playing snooker and visiting each other's digs, and made the long trip home together when the club allowed them a weekend with their families.

Neil says that the hardest time for both of them was returning to the club after their first Christmas break. For much of that trip they had both been utterly miserable, wanting to be back in Newcastle. The sadness soon passed. Within a week they were back in the swing of things – training, playing and doing all the jobs that are part of life for a football trainee. There was the senior players' boots to be cleaned and polished, kit to be washed, dressing-rooms to be swept out and the medical room to be disinfected. And there were times when they were simply too tired to be homesick.

The training was harder than anything they had been used to. Alan loved it, if it involved a ball. He wasn't so keen on the running – and there seemed to be a great deal of that. The stamina required to play football at the highest level doesn't come without hard work. Nobody made Alan more aware of that than Southampton's goalkeeper, Peter Shilton. He was 38, old enough to be Alan's father, but he was still England's number one. Shilton was a fanatical trainer, who was always prepared to stay out on the pitch a bit longer to work on some aspect of his game. Once he challenged Alan to a penalty contest and saved five out of five, an example that left Alan deeply impressed.

Another character at the club was Mark Dennis. He was a skilful left-back with a powerful shot, but he had a terrible disciplinary record. Despite his reputation as a wild man he had a good relationship with the trainees and with Alan in particular. At Christmas it's traditional for the professional players to give the trainees a cash tip. In the mid 1980s £20 was the going rate, but Dennis decided to up the stakes for Alan. He put £1 under one cup and a £50 note under another and invited Alan to go for broke. The thought of getting his hands on what amounted to two weeks' wages was just too great a temptation and Alan took the chance. He guessed wrong, but Dennis gave him £20 anyway.

Above all, though, there was the football. The youth side, in which Alan quickly staked his claim to the number nine shirt, was a bit special in 1986. A tall, slightly gangly 18-year-old from Guernsey, Matthew Le Tissier, was reckoned to be the most outstanding talent and was already turning out for the first team. Rod Wallace, whose elder brother Danny played up front for the seniors, was another attacking star of Merrington's exciting youth team. Individually they were good; together they made a lethal combination. Chris Nicholl, who had succeeded Lawrie McMenemy as Southampton's manager, would say later of that youth team: 'Wallace had the speed off the mark and agility. Le Tissier had the class and the cleverness on the ball. Shearer had the strength.'

Alan had something else, too, something that Merrington was becoming increasingly aware of: 'He had a very positive approach. He found his feet very quickly. Once the lads had been at the club around six months I tried to encourage them to give feedback, to talk about what they were doing. Alan was always willing to say what he thought, never nervous to say that we weren't defending well enough, or getting in good crosses. But he could always listen to advice.'

Alan had a terrific first season with Southampton. He scored 31 goals for the youth side, a tally unmatched by anyone else in the club. He had settled into the routine quickly, and he was loving every minute of it. By the end of that 1986/87 season Merrington had seen enough to be convinced that Alan was ready to step straight up to the first team. Pitching a teenager into the deep end is a risky business. It can make or break a young player. But Merrington was confident that Alan had the maturity to handle whatever might be thrown at him. During the summer break in 1987 he talked with Chris Nicholl about moving Alan into the senior ranks.

Nicholl wasn't keen to do this. His first impressions

were that Alan was very strong, and that he had a large backside – both encouraging signs. Alan had by this time grown to practically his full height and weight and was developing the ideal physique for a striker – compact and powerful with a low centre of gravity for speed on the turn. But Nicholl felt that his first touch and left-foot control were still not up to scratch.

So, now the work started to get serious. Merrington convinced Nicholl that Alan was worth the extra effort and the Geordie lad responded, staying behind for extra practice when his mates had left to shower and change. The coaching staff kicked and threw balls at him from all directions and angles to make him improve his first-time control. They yelled at him to use that big backside and stick it out 'like Kenny Dalglish' to hold off defenders. Alan worked tirelessly on bettering the strength and the timing of his left foot, hitting balls over and over again off every part of it. Progress was frustratingly slow at first, then it seemed to speed up. He thrived on the attention, determined to master the skills that would get him that break into the first side.

Alan still played for the youth team, but as the 1987/88 season wore on he was more often turning out for the senior reserves, for the first time pitching himself against men rather than boys. It made him reasonably confident that the club would take him on as a professional at the end of the season, when his two years as a YTS trainee would be up. He knew others wouldn't be so lucky. Southampton would turn down many of the lads he had worked and played with for the last 18 months, their dreams of a life in football in shreds.

In February 1988 Alan's progress was recognized. He was called up to the England Under-17 team for the match against the Republic of Ireland at Stoke City. It was the biggest game of his career so far, his first appearance in his country's colours. His parents were there to watch him, so were Jack Hixon and Dave Merrington. And Alan didn't let them down. It was a bit of a scruffy goal – an instinctive toe-poke in the penalty area from a flicked-down corner – but it was a goal all the same. As every striker says, they all count, whether they're tap-ins from two yards or screamers from outside the box.

It was a proud moment. England won the game 2–1 and the name Alan Shearer had for the first time appeared on the scoresheet for a national side. Everyone realized that it wouldn't be the last.

In the stands Merrington told Hixon how he'd been pushing to get Alan into the first team. 'He's on fire,' he said. 'He's ready.' At long last – so it seemed to the impatient Alan – Nicholl agreed.

Six weeks later Alan made his first-team debut. He came on for the last 10 minutes as a sub against Chelsea at Stamford Bridge, not enough time to make much of an impact. Afterwards he was given no indication about when he would get another chance. Then, on 8 April, only a couple of hours before kick-off, Nicholl called for Alan and casually told him to get ready. Danny Wallace had failed a late fitness test and Alan would be in the starting line-up to face Arsenal.

There was hardly enough time to be nervous, which was just as well because there was plenty to be nervous about. This was the deep end all right. Arsenal were way above Southampton in the league table. They were a club chasing for honours with a squad stuffed full of star players, many of them internationals. At least it was at the Dell, a ground that Alan had already come to know and love. Small by the standards of the top clubs, the Dell has a slightly old-fashioned feel. The closeness of the spectators to the pitch helps to generate an excitement that few venues can match. The voices of the fans ring out so clearly that the players can hear their rolling Hampshire accents.

What happened that day became part of footballing history, and not just because the Saints pulled off a surprise 4-2 win over the Gunners. Alan had marked his first full appearance in the most incredible manner possible. He scored a hat trick.

The game was only five minutes' old when he struck first. He still hadn't had time to take in the enormity of the occasion when he found himself running to get on the end of a cross hit to the far post. In the eyes of the Arsenal defence, he simply turned up from nowhere. Alan's stretching header squeezed between John Lukic's legs and rolled over the line.

He couldn't believe it. Neither could the South-ampton fans who had turned up more in hope than in expectation of a win over the mighty Arsenal. And that was only the beginning.

The second goal was equally straightforward. A one–two around the penalty area with Colin Clarke on the wing, followed by a well-driven first-time shot that gave Lukic no chance. The Arsenal defenders, Gus Caesar and Michael Thomas, were given a furious tongue-lashing from their exposed goalkeeper after that one!

The Dell instantly came alive, delighted to see this unknown 17-year-old trainee tearing the Arsenal defence into ribbons. The ground rocked with their cheers and chants as the delighted fans willed the youngster on to even more glory.

It came early in the second half. Another lung-bursting run took Alan between the Gunners' central defenders to connect with Colin Clarke's cross. His shot hit the bar, but he was the first to respond to the rebound, stabbing it home from short range. He set off on a celebration run of pure joy, a sprint that left his jubilant team-mates trailing in his wake until the tiredness in his legs overcame the excitement.

The reporters in the press box and in newsrooms around Britain were left furiously checking their record books, trying to discover when something like this had happened before. In fact Alan was the youngest ever hat-trick scorer in what was then the First Division, and the youngest player ever to have hit three goals on his first full appearance in the English league. For the first – but by no means the last – time, the photographs and headlines on the back pages of the newspapers the next day were devoted to the goal-scoring exploits of Alan Shearer.

He didn't complete the match. That last celebration run finished him off. He had run his heart out for an hour and there was nothing left in his tanks. Nicholl wisely brought him off, to a roar from the Southampton faithful that made the Dell shake. Exhausted, but elated, Alan was brought down to earth with a crash when Merrington reminded him that it was his turn to get the kit washed that weekend!

Nothing though, not even those muddy shirts and

shorts, could dampen Alan's spirits. He had been given the match ball, autographed by all the players. This trophy would have had pride of place in most footballers' collections, but Alan unhesitatingly gave it to the people who had done most to make it happen – his parents.

Perhaps more importantly, Alan had also been given the respect and admiration of his team-mates, the professionals whom he'd watched and learned from over the past two seasons. It was one thing to read the flattering reports in the papers, and another to hear his name ringing around the Dell, but when players like Peter Shilton or Jimmy Case sang his praises it really meant something.

Case was then the club captain and an enormously experienced ball-winning midfielder. He had won practically all the game's honours during eight years with Liverpool. He had seen most things in the game, but in Alan he knew he'd seen something special. 'Arsenal just couldn't handle his freshness and enthusiasm,' is how he later described the moment. 'Other youngsters have made bright starts and then disappeared without trace. What set him apart from the rest was his attitude. He was old before his time and even playing for the youth team he had developed a competitive streak.'

But the youth team era was over now. Four days

after the hat trick Alan signed his first professional contract. By the standards of later years that first pay packet was pretty small, though it was a good deal better than the £25 a week YTS money he was used to. But all that really mattered was that he had made it. All his life he'd wanted to be a professional footballer, thought about nothing else, dreamed about nothing else – and worked hard to make it happen. Now it had. But if there was satisfaction in the achievement, there was also growing ambition. He'd come this far. What was to stop him going further?

CHAPTER FOUR

Shearer for England!

T HE NEW SEASON just couldn't come quickly enough for Alan. It would be his first as a professional. He was on a high, his confidence boosted by being called up to the England Under-18 team during the summer. But he soon discovered that even that didn't guarantee a regular place in the Southampton team.

Under Chris Nicholl, the club had built up a squad that had many attacking players. Nicholl strengthened it further just before the 1988/89 season began by buying a new striker. Paul Rideout was only 24, but he had eight years of league experience behind him, including the last three spent at Bari, one of Italy's top clubs. Nicholl had bought him not just because of his proven goal-scoring record, but also because of his control and first touch. Rideout could bring Southampton's other gifted forwards into the game in a way that Alan had yet to master.

Alan made only 10 league appearances that season and failed to score in any of them. It was frustrating sitting on the bench or playing in the reserves, especially when he saw the impact his former youth team-mates Le Tissier and Rod Wallace were making. But it only spurred him on and made him determined to train even harder.

He found a soul-mate in Tim Flowers, a goalkeeper who had come to Southampton from Wolverhampton Wanderers. Tim shared the same outlook at Alan. He had an unshakeable faith in his own ability as shown by the message on his answerphone: 'Safest hands in soccer.' He also had an insatiable appetite for training. Like Peter Shilton, who had now moved on to Derby County, Tim never stopped working at his game.

Neil Ruddock was another new Southampton player who would become a close friend. He was a larger than life character who knew how to have a good time and who never stopped taking the mickey out of Alan. Neil had come from Millwall and always said that Southampton had spotted him after he had marked Alan out of a reserves game, a version of events that Alan disputed.

Both Tim and Neil would remain friends even

when all three had left Southampton. Later, Tim and Alan would be reunited at Blackburn Rovers, and they would all be called up to play for England under Terry Venables.

But by far Alan's closest companion at this time was Lainya, a dark-haired, blue-eyed local girl. They had first met in a wine bar in 1987 (an outing that Dave Merrington would certainly have disapproved of – if he'd known). Lainya had never been to a match and didn't know the slightest thing about football. As Alan has said since, 'She certainly wasn't after my money.' He was still a trainee when they first started going out and Lainya's pay packet was rather larger than his.

If Alan had ever questioned signing for Southampton rather than his beloved Newcastle, the 1988/89 season convinced him that he had made the right decision. He might not have been getting a place in the starting eleven, but at least he was still playing for a First Division club. While Southampton finished in a respectable mid-table position, earning praise for their attractive and entertaining football, Newcastle were relegated.

Much had changed at Newcastle since Alan's first trial there. Waddle and Beardsley had been snapped up by other clubs. Now their brightest young star, Paul Gascoigne, had gone to Tottenham. The club was hit by troubles on and off the pitch and the new manager, Jim Smith, was unable to stop them. Alan was, of course, committed to Southampton. Even so, Newcastle's results were always the first he'd look for on Saturday afternoons.

Alan's progress at this stage was steady rather than spectacular. In his second professional season, though, he started to show the form that made him impossible to leave out. Danny Wallace left Southampton to join Manchester United, which made it a little easier to get into the team, although Paul Rideout remained the first choice for the number nine shirt. Alan made 26 league appearances that season, some from the substitutes' bench. Although the goals didn't exactly come flooding in, his name did occasionally appear on the score-sheet.

Alan's final tally for the league season was three, a number that didn't reflect either the effort he was making or his all-round contribution to a very successful team. Rideout hadn't done a great deal better – 7 goals from 31 games. However, Le Tissier and Rod Wallace hit the net 38 times between them and hogged the headlines that year. It was one of Southampton's best-ever seasons, too. They finished seventh in the league, six places above Manchester United. Only the runaway winners, Liverpool, scored more goals.

Alan first really came to be noticed outside

Southampton in the 1989/90 season. As Dave Merrington recalls: 'When he started to go away on England trips, we knew we were going to have problems. It wouldn't take long for anyone who worked with him to realize how good he was.'

Ray Harford was one outsider who already had a fair inkling of Alan's potential. When manager of Luton, one of his scouts, former Arsenal centre-back Terry Mancini, had tipped him off about this young Southampton striker. Now Harford was managing Wimbledon, but he was also involved with the England Under-21 set-up. It was through this that he had the chance to see Alan close up.

Alan made his first full Under-21 appearance on 13 November 1990, against the Republic of Ireland away from home. He'd had his first taste of football at this level a month before, coming on as a sub for the last 12 minutes in a game against Poland, which England lost 1–0. Now, in the starting line-up for the first time (alongside club team-mates Rod Wallace and Jason Dodd), he was determined to make the most of his opportunity.

His first game in international colours – three years previously with the Under-17s – had been against the Republic of Ireland. He had scored then, but this time he went one better, getting two in a confident 3–0 victory.

An Under-21 cap was no guarantee of a place in the full England side, but Alan knew perfectly well that most of the international seniors had come through the Under-21 ranks. Gary Lineker, England's hero in the World Cup in Italy the summer before, was a notable exception.

International football places different demands on a player from club football. He has to be able to learn quickly, to adapt to new systems of play alongside relative strangers as team-mates. He has to be capable of performing in front of foreign, and sometimes hostile, crowds, hundreds of miles from home after long hours of travelling and being cooped up in hotels.

Alan came through this test with flying colours. His eagerness to learn, his enthusiasm on the pitch, and the mature attitude with which he faced every new experience made a lasting impression on the England Under-21 coaches. During 1991 his name would automatically be the first on the Under-21 teamsheet.

Things were beginning to take off at Southampton, too. Paul Rideout was getting so few first-team games in the 1990/91 season that he was loaned out to Swindon Town. The goals still weren't coming in significant numbers but the style Southampton was using meant Alan often played alone up front, laying off chances for Le Tissier and Wallace. This style, which had proved so successful the year before, was less effective this season, though. Southampton slumped to 14th in the league, a long way behind the thrills and excitement at the top where Arsenal had snatched the title from Liverpool in the closing seconds of the final game. Southampton's lack of form resulted in manager Chris Nicholl being fired and replaced by Ian Branfoot. Alan was sorry to see Nicholl go and made a special point of ringing his former boss to thank him for all his help and to wish him all the best for the future. It was a gesture that was much appreciated by Nicholl.

For Alan the real breakthrough came in the summer of 1991 when he captained the England Under-21 team in a UEFA tournament held in Toulon in France. It was a triumph for the England team, which under coach Ray Harford won all four matches. But it was a personal triumph for Alan, who had celebrated being awarded the captaincy with a hat trick against Mexico. He had gone on to score seven goals in total, including a brilliant winner in the final against France. It had taken him just over 3 years to notch up 10 league goals for Southampton. However, in an England shirt it seemed he couldn't stop scoring.

When he came back from Toulon he found Southampton buzzing with rumours that he would be called up to the full England squad. Under their new manager, Graham Taylor, the England players were about to leave for a tour of Australia and New Zealand. The rumours turned out to be untrue, which was a huge relief for Lainya, if not for Alan. The tour dates clashed with their wedding, and she had no doubt what Alan's response would have been if the call had come through. Their best man was Neil Maddison, a friend since Alan's days in the youth team.

Alan had to wait a while yet for his first senior cap, but the way he started the 1991/92 season left those watching certain it would come soon. Branfoot favoured a more direct approach than Nicholl, so Alan found himself pushed further forward and used as the target of Southampton's attacks, rather than just as a part in them. It was a system of play that was sometimes unpopular with the Saints' fans. They thought Le Tissier's skills were being wasted, but it gave Alan more of a chance to shine.

He was by now a very different player from the 17-year-old who had scored that incredible first-time hat trick. He was not just stronger and faster, but far more skilful. The left foot packed a punch that was not far off the right's for pace and accuracy. There was power and subtlety in his heading, and he was developing a confident first touch and the ability to retain the ball under pressure.

But in some ways he was still the Newcastle junior school kid who had to be played in midfield because he wanted to take every corner, every throw-in and every free kick. Alan's commitment on the pitch was total. He would chase after every pass, follow in every shot in case of a rebound, throw his head in where the boots were flying, and do more than his fair share of defensive duties. For the first time, though, he was being given the freedom to make goal-scoring his number-one priority.

Goals weren't easy to come by as Southampton struggled to make the transition to their new system of play. Some familiar faces were missing. Jimmy Case had gone to Bournemouth. Rod Wallace had left for Leeds, who, just up from the Second Division would go on to win the championship. For much of the season the Saints were in the relegation zone and Alan had to work hard to convert the few chances he was given into the goals they needed to stay in the top flight.

He made good use of his first chance within two minutes of the season starting. Alan raced to collect a throw-in from Jeff Kenna and then unleashed a snap shot from 20 yards that left Tottenham keeper Eric Thorstvedt clutching at thin air. The celebration run that followed that goal was not just for himself. A few minutes before the kick-off his mother had rung to tell him that his father had placed a bet on him being Southampton's first goal-scorer.

The enthusiasm, the work-rate and the steadily increasing flow of goals made a call-up to the full England squad a dream that seemed ever more likely to come true. Through the rest of 1991 Alan had to be patient, with 3 more goals for the Under-21s, in which his personal tally rose to a staggering 13 goals from 11 full appearances. As 1991 turned into 1992 he grew closer to fulfilling his dream. First came the call-up to the England squad, and the chance to rub shoulders on the training field with the finest players in the country, many of whom had been his idols just a few years before. Then, on 19 February 1992, he was in – to play against France in a friendly at Wembley.

England were looking to build on the success of the 1990 World Cup in Italy. Then they had missed reaching the final only after a heart-breaking, semi-final penalty shoot-out against West Germany. The first test facing manager Graham Taylor, who had succeeded Bobby Robson after Italia 90, was the 1992 European Championships in Sweden.

Taylor, in some ways like Southampton's Branfoot, was a believer in fast, direct football. He instinctively liked the look of this powerful Southampton striker who covered a lot of ground and shot on sight. The England attack was based around Gary Lineker, a very different type of player from Alan. Taylor wanted a stand-in for when Lineker was injured, but he was also looking for a new striking partner for the England captain. Alan was only one of several he was considering.

The friendly against France was a break from the European Championships qualifiers. Taylor used the game to experiment with his attacking options, partnering Alan with David Hirst of Sheffield Wednesday. Hirst had scored 24 league goals in 1990/91 and had broken into the England squad on their tour of the Pacific, scoring in a 2–0 victory over New Zealand. It would be only his second full cap, making this one of the most inexperienced attacking partnerships England had ever fielded.

Alan had a good record of scoring on first appearances and it was even better after this match. Midway through a tense first-half, England's tall centre-back Mark Wright leapt above the French defence to head down Nigel Clough's corner. From the edge of the six-yard box, Alan turned and slammed a shoulder-high, right-foot shot into the goal.

He was already bursting with pride at simply being chosen, the schoolboy dream of being picked for his country having come true at the age of only 21. The goal made it all the more special. And to top it all, this was Wembley! Not the usual league ground with a few fans where the Under-21 games had been played, but Wembley, the home of English football. It was only a friendly, so it wasn't quite packed to the rafters. But to score at Wembley for England and to hear the crowd chanting his name for the first time gave Alan a buzz that he just had to repeat. The second-half, in which his header on to the bar was stabbed home by Lineker (on for the substituted Hirst) passed in a blur.

Alan was given little time to dwell on the thrill of that first international. He was back at Southampton the following day, preparing for the next league match. The Saints were struggling for every point in an increasingly nerve-racking battle against relegation. No club ever wants to go down, but there was an especially good reason to stay up that year. The FA Premier League was about to become the new top division and large amounts of money were at stake. To be left behind in this race would be disastrous for a relatively small club like Southampton.

They made it but, although the fans were delighted to have avoided the drop, they had not taken to Branfoot or the new style of play. Alan was the team's hero that season. He played in all but one of the league programme of 42 games and his 13 goals made him the Saints' top scorer.

He was in demand now. Other managers were sizing him up and wondering what Southampton would let him go for. Ray Harford had approached the club when he was manager at Wimbledon, but found the asking-price too high.

Harford had since left Wimbledon to join Blackburn Rovers. This might have looked like a step down because Blackburn were a Second Division club who hadn't won anything since before the First World War. But a local millionaire businessman, Jack Walker, had recently taken control of the club and was sparing no expense to make Blackburn one of the strongest clubs in the land. He had already pulled off one master stroke by persuading Kenny Dalglish out of retirement to manage the side, with Harford as his right-hand man.

Harford wasted no time in letting Dalglish know that Alan was the player they needed to sign if they were going to cut it with the big boys. Alan was flattered by Rovers' interest but he had no intention of stepping down a division. If Blackburn were going to get their man, they would have to make sure of promotion first. Indeed, they would later snatch the last place in the new Premier League through the play-offs.

With the league season over, Alan's priority now was to secure a place in the England squad for the European Championships. He wasn't chosen for the game against Czechoslovakia, where Taylor picked Mark Hateley and John Barnes to play up front, but he was in against the C.I.S., the countries that had previously been known as the U.S.S.R. This time he was paired with Lineker, and he learned at first hand the uncertainties of international football. Only three of the team that kicked off in Moscow that night had been with him in the starting line-up against France. It was a scrappy game, that ended 2−2 with Alan on the bench, having been substituted in the second-half by Nigel Clough.

The game left him very unsure about his chances of making the European Championships squad, but when the 20 names were made public, his was one of them. At 21 he was getting the chance to play in a major international tournament, alongside many of the world's greatest footballers.

Alan played only a small part in what would go down in footballing history as one of England's most unsuccessful tournament appearances. He was on the bench for the opening game against Denmark, for which Taylor chose Arsenal striker Alan Smith to partner Lineker. That game ended goal-less, as did the second against France, when Alan started in preference to Smith. He was back on the bench, with Smith, for the crucial third match against the host-nation, Sweden. This time Taylor decided to play Lineker alone up front.

David Platt took England into the lead in the first-half, but the Swedes soon struck back to equalize. Midway through the second half Taylor made the decision that left the football world reeling, taking off Lineker and bringing on Smith. Within a few minutes Tomas Brolin had scored for Sweden and England were out of the European Championships.

Alan Smith remembers their return to England as a sad affair, with not an autograph-hunter in sight at Luton airport. After Italia 90 the England players had been treated to an open-bus parade through streets crowded with cheering supporters. This time there were only the cameras and tape-recorders of the press surrounding Taylor and bombarding him with questions. 'It wasn't so bad for us players,' Smith pointed out. 'We were off on our holidays, and could push the tournament to the back of our minds as we looked forward to a new season.'

Alan was looking forward to his holidays, too. It had been a long, hard season with more than 60 games – if you included the Zenith Data Systems Cup, in which Southampton had reached the final, only to be beaten by Nottingham Forest. And he had fatherhood to look forward to, with his wife Lainya due to give birth in September.

But the summer break was going to be a short one. Blackburn Rovers, having secured their place in the Premier League, had made their move. Their offer was one Southampton had to take seriously – £3 million in money, plus the £300,000-striker, David Speedie. If Alan accepted the offer, it would make him the most expensive player in England.

CHAPTER FIVE

Down but not Out

O F ALL THE OBSTACLES in the way of a
promising young player, two are famously
difficult to overcome. The first is the move – from a
small club to a big one and with a price tag on your
head that has to be justified quickly. The second is
the serious injury – how you cope physically and
mentally with being out of the game for a long time.
Alan confronted – and conquered – both obstacles
in his first year at Blackburn.

From the first approach to the signing of contracts,
the record-breaking transfer took only a few days.
Following the same gut instinct that had first taken
him to Southampton, Alan felt almost immediately
that Blackburn would be a good move. Several factors
influenced him, but one thing clinched it – Kenny
Dalglish.

Dalglish had been one of Alan's most important

role models. Chris Nicholl had urged him to take notice of Dalglish's skills, particularly the way he shielded the ball and created scoring opportunities with his speed and control on the turn. Alan had taken all these on board as well as recognizing that Dalglish's burning will to win was an important part of his incredible success both as a player and as a manager.

This was something they had in common. Perhaps this was why they took to each other from the start. Alan and Lainya travelled up to the old mill town in Lancashire to visit the club and its surroundings. Marina Dalglish took Lainya under her wing, while Kenny showed Alan around and answered his questions.

On the long journey back to Southampton Alan mulled over what he had seen and heard. He had been impressed by Blackburn's obvious determination to reach the highest levels. They had only scraped into the newly formed Premiership through the play-offs, but already they were aiming for the top. A Southampton-style struggle against relegation was out of the question, not with Jack Walker's millions available to someone like Dalglish. All around him Alan had seen evidence of how Blackburn Rovers were being transformed. The squad was being strengthened. The training facilities were being improved, and the old Ewood Park ground was being rebuilt to standards that would be the envy of any club in the Premiership. He was encouraged, too, by the prospect of training and playing under Blackburn's first-team coach, Ray Harford, the man who had made him captain of the England Under-21s.

Most of all, though, Alan and Lainya had been impressed by the warmth of their welcome. Here was a club that would do anything to help them settle into their new home. For Lainya, about to become a mother for the first time, this was especially important. Nobody would do more for them than Kenny and Marina Dalglish, who had been through much the same experience 15 years before when Kenny had joined Liverpool from Celtic. Dalglish saw this role as part and parcel of a manager's job. He would do the same for any new player, but from the start he had a special affection for the young Shearers.

Alan had asked Dalglish for 24 hours to think about the move. His mind was made up even before they reached Southampton. Lainya agreed. Minutes after arriving home he was on the phone to tell Dalglish, 'I'd love to sign for you.' On 27 July 1992, Alan Shearer became a Blackburn Rovers player.

The press response to the transfer was greater than anything Alan had expected – or was used to. Many journalists wondered if Blackburn Rovers had more money than sense. This Shearer lad wasn't bad, they reckoned, but he didn't have much of a record as a goal-scorer – only 23 in 118 league appearances. This was crazy money, they said, and nothing good would come of it.

People also questioned Alan's decision to go to Blackburn. Manchester United had been after him, they said, but he had turned them down because Rovers had offered more money. In fact, Alan had only been officially approached by Blackburn. But that didn't stop the newspapers making wild estimates about his salary, which in turn led to a club grounds-man giving Alan a nickname that would stick: Billy Big Pockets.

To cap it all, Alan knew that many Blackburn fans were not behind him either. He would be replacing David Speedie up front. David was a tough and experienced little striker whose 23 goals the season before had done much to get Rovers into the Premier-ship. He was a big favourite with the Ewood Park crowd and banners calling for his return were held up when Alan turned out in pre-season friendlies for his new club.

The calm way in which Alan handled the press attention impressed his new employers. He told reporters that the worst pressure he was under was his new baby crying all night, that if you couldn't handle pressure you shouldn't be in the game anyway. The answers were clear and direct, but they gave little away. Alan knew perfectly well that he was at an important point in his career, midway between being a very promising player and a really great one. He also knew that the only way to silence the critics and the fans was to deliver the goods on the pitch.

His first 45 minutes were the worst. Blackburn were making their Premiership debut at Selhurst Park. In the dressing-room at half-time, Alan sat with his elbows on his knees, staring into space. He was listening to Harford talking through their first-half performance and sounding not best pleased with it. Alan knew he'd had a poor half, never quite getting into a game that was being played at a furious pace. Already he was imagining what the headlines for the £3.3-million man would be the following day.

If his confidence was shaken, he showed no sign of it when the first clear-cut chance came his way early in the second-half. A long ball up from the back, a nod down by striking partner Mike Newell, and Alan, seeing Palace keeper Nigel Martyn a few yards off his line, unleashed a first-time, right-foot volley from just outside the box. The ball flew over the backpeddling Martyn's outstretched fingers and dipped wickedly, almost skimming the underside of the crossbar, as it crashed into the roof of the net.

That was a special moment. Not just any old goal. His first for Blackburn, true. But also another in his extraordinary collection of first-appearance scores. A great goal, a brilliant one. That moment would be shown over and over again on *Match of the Day* that night, from different angles and in slow motion. It was an instant certainty for the goal-of-the-month short list.

Later in the second-half, Alan converted a second, rather easier, chance. The game ended in a 3–3 draw and the name of only one player on everyone's lips. The Premiership, which had lost Paul Gascoigne and David Platt to Italy, and Gary Lineker to Japan, had found its new star attraction.

Blackburn made a sizzling start to the season and nobody was hotter than Alan, banging in goals at a furious rate. At Ewood Park on 3 October Rovers met Norwich, at that stage riding high at the top of the table. Blackburn tore them apart, winning 7–1 in a game which had the commentators drooling over Alan's speed, strength and power of shot. But he also demonstrated a gentle touch that day, producing a fine little chip to beat Bryan Gunn from 30 yards. That was a leaf straight from the Kenny Dalglish book.

Alan settled in quickly. His new team-mates soon learned that however much Billy Big Pockets cost, he was prepared to work for it. His willingness to chase after everything, and to do something useful when he got it, made every ball sent his way a threat to the opposition.

Most of the passes he received were more than just hopeful. Alan was thriving on the fast and accurate service he was getting from the wings, from Stuart Ripley on the right and Jason Wilcox on the left. He was always alert, too, for the perceptive long through-ball from midfield, invariably played by veteran Gordon Cowans. Alan's England team-mate, David Platt, once said that his ambition in football was to make a run that wasn't spotted by Cowans. Although near the end of a long career, Cowans still had a lovely touch and vision.

The Rovers team was a good mixture of old and young heads, long-servers and newcomers. Some, like Wilcox and defender David May, had served their apprenticeships with the club and were just breaking through to the first team. Others dated back to the pre-Dalglish era – like veteran centre-back Steve Moran, goalkeeper Bobby Mimms and midfielder Mark Atkins. And there were the new signings – Ripley from Middlesbrough, Tim Sherwood from Norwich, and Alan's regular strike partner, Mike Newell from Everton. That 7–1 thrashing of Norwich was a clear sign that under Dalglish and Harford they were being welded together into a team that could seriously threaten the giant sides from the nearby cities of Manchester and Liverpool.

Alan's goals and Blackburn's form strengthened his claim for the England number nine shirt. Now that Gary Lineker had retired from international football, Alan had become the natural candidate to lead the England attack in the qualifying campaign for the 1994 World Cup in the USA.

Taylor picked him alongside Nigel Clough for the first international of the season – a friendly, away to Spain, which England lost 1–0. Ian Wright of Arsenal was his striking partner – the fourth one in Alan's five games for England – when the World Cup qualifiers got under way against Norway at Wembley. The result was a disappointing 1–1 draw, with David Platt getting England's goal. Taylor kept faith with Alan and Ian for the next match, against Turkey at Wembley. Alan rewarded him with a goal, though it was the double strike from an inspired Paul Gascoigne that made the headlines.

Up to Christmas the season couldn't have gone better for Alan. Blackburn were riding high in the Premiership and he was at the head of the goal-scorers' table. But on Boxing Day the good luck suddenly, and terribly, ran out.

Blackburn were playing Leeds at Ewood Park.

Near the end of the first-half, Alan, lining up a left-foot shot, had his right leg knocked away by a tackle. He felt a twinge instantly, but got to his feet thinking nothing of it. It was a perfectly fair tackle and the pain no worse than many knocks he'd taken before. A few minutes later, he even scored. He hit the net again in the second half – his 16th in 21 league appearances and his 22nd of the season. But there was clearly something wrong. A long chase down the middle came to an abrupt halt when Alan felt his right knee give way. He carried on for a few more minutes, but with the game practically won and the twinges more painful, he signalled to the bench. They thought it was a cartilage problem, nasty enough, but not too serious. He was advised to rest completely for 10 days. Alan obeyed his instructions to the letter and on the 11th day turned up for training. The knee went instantly.

The important thing now was to find out what was the matter. A weary process of X-rays and examinations eventually revealed what everyone had begun to dread. Alan had ruptured the cruciate ligament in his right knee. This is one of the most serious injuries a footballer can suffer, and one from which many never recover fully. At best it meant probably a year out of the game. At worst it meant the end of his career.

Alan now needed a tricky operation. Even if it was successful, the battle would be less than half won. First, he would have to wait for the ligament to heal. Then he would have to build up the wasted muscles around the knee, to ease the strain on the ligament as much as possible. All this would require a lonely and punishing training schedule in the weights room, knowing that few recovered to their previous levels of speed and strength.

The mental scars left by a serious injury are often deeper than the physical ones. Like all good strikers Alan was brave, not afraid to stick his foot or his head into harm's way. Would he still be the same if he did manage to recover his fitness, now that he knew his career could be ended in the split second it takes to mistime a tackle?

The days turned into weeks, then weeks into months. Time dragged on for Alan. He missed the day-to-day life of a footballer, joking with the lads in the dressing-room or on the training field, the celebrations after a good result. Most of all, he missed football. He couldn't even kick a ball around his garden, let alone Ewood Park or Wembley in front of tens of thousands.

Recovering from a long-term injury is the toughest battle a professional player can face. It is made all the harder by being fought far away from the cheers of the crowd and the glowing headlines. Alan knew it was going to be difficult, but as he went under the surgeon's knife in February 1993 he had already resolved how he was going to deal with it. He was going to stay positive, to continue to believe that he was meant for more than early retirement, and to work like hell to return to full fitness.

The operation was a success. The first hurdle had been overcome. Now it would be three months before he could manage so much as a light jog. In that time he saw Manchester United swing the season around by buying Eric Cantona from Leeds and then romp home to their first championship in 26 years. He watched Arsenal beat Sheffield Wednesday 2−1 in the Coca-Cola Cup final, a game that was to be repeated right down to the score-line in the FA Cup final a few weeks later. And he saw England held to a 2−2 draw by Holland at Wembley, and then beaten 2−0 by Norway in Oslo, to leave their World Cup hopes shattered.

Blackburn finished the season fourth, one point behind Norwich and three behind Aston Villa, an excellent result for their first season in the top flight. Scottish-striker Kevin Gallacher had been bought from Coventry to fill Alan's place and he had done a good job up front alongside Mike Newell. But the thought that ran through everyone's minds was what would have happened if Shearer hadn't been injured? Not just for Blackburn, but for England, too.

Even though he had played in only half the league's programme of 42 games, Alan's 16 goals put him fifth on the list of the Premiership's goal-scorers. Teddy Sheringham, who had moved to Tottenham from Nottingham Forest, had topped the list with 22, ahead of QPR's Les Ferdinand (20), Wimbledon's Dean Holdsworth (19) and Coventry's Mick Quinn (17).

In Alan's absence the striker who attracted most talk in the second-half of that season was not even in the Premiership, though he soon would be. Andy Cole, a 21-year-old former Arsenal trainee with struggling Bristol City, had gone to Newcastle for £1.75 million late in the season. He had fired in 12 goals in as many games to help them win the First Division title.

Alan's home team, after years of decline, were going through a Blackburn-style transformation. The club was now under the control of Sir John Hall who, like Jack Walker, was a wealthy man with an ambition to win. One thing Sir John had succeeded in doing that everyone in football had failed to achieve was to persuade Kevin Keegan back into the game.

Alan could well remember the impact Keegan had made 10 years earlier as a player. His return to the club as manager was greeted with even more excitement in Newcastle. Immediately he'd turned the team round, from scrabbling at the bottom to winning promotion at a gallop. Andy Cole was the bright new star of a team that would make Premiership life even more interesting in the coming season.

The only thing Alan would let himself think through that long, hard summer was that he would soon be out there, facing Newcastle, Manchester United and the rest. By July he was running again, working out daily in the gym, pumping weights like a madman. His progress astounded the Blackburn staff, who found that far from having to encourage him they had to hold him back, to stop him from doing too much too soon. By August Alan was hopping on his right leg up the steps on the Ewood Park terraces, a display that left his team-mates shaking their heads with disbelief and admiration.

Dalglish was so impressed by Alan's progress that he decided to bring him back into the squad for a pre-season warm-up tour in Ireland. Quite rightly, Harford reckoned that it was too soon, that Alan wasn't ready. But Dalglish wanted to give Alan a lift. He wanted him back in the swing of things, mixing with the lads even if he was a bit rusty and far from match fit. Dalglish also wanted to give Alan a taste of playing again, just enough to get him over any barrier that might be lingering in his mind. He thought that it would be better to do that away from the blaze of publicity that would surround a Premiership match. As far as Alan was concerned he was in Ireland more for the ride than anything else. He had no inkling of what was coming when, with about 10 minutes remaining of one match, Dalglish casually turned to him on the bench and said quietly, 'Go on, have a game.'

It was just a little taste but it had a sweet flavour. In those 10 minutes Alan scored twice. He still wasn't up to the demands of 90 minutes in the Premiership, but now there was no doubt that he soon would be. Anyone who could get back on to the pitch, *and* score, within eight months of rupturing a cruciate ligament, wasn't going to take long to reach peak fitness.

Alan was raring to go, but Dalglish held him back for the first few weeks of the season, limiting his appearances to second-half substitutions. He made his Premiership return on 18 August, 236 days after the injury. He ran on for the last few minutes of the game against Norwich to a huge cheer from the Ewood Park fans. There was another great welcome from the Newcastle fans when he came off the bench at St James' Park a few days later. That was a moment Alan appreciated, although he showed no mercy to his home team, cracking in a second-half goal in a fiercely fought 1–1 draw.

His first game in the starting line-up was on 21 September. It was the home leg of a second-round Coca-Cola Cup-tie against Bournemouth. Blackburn won 1–0, with the goal supplied by Alan. His full Premiership return came four days later at home to Sheffield Wednesday. This time Blackburn were held to a 1–1 draw. Yet again, it was Alan who had hit the net.

Alan Shearer was back with a vengeance, every bit as fast, strong and brave as before. He was picking up exactly where he had left off, scoring goals by the bucketful.

Graham Taylor had been keeping a close eye on his recovery. After seeing him knock in two during a ruthless demolition of struggling Swindon Town, he called Alan back to the national squad. England were preparing for a World Cup qualifier against Holland that they had to win if they were to stand any real chance of going to USA 94. Alan had started only two Premiership games all season, and he was a long way behind strikers such as Andy Cole and Ian Wright in the goal-scorers' table. Nevertheless, when the team was announced, he was in.

Alan's delight at winning back his England place was balanced by the realization of how difficult a task they faced – to win away from home against one of the best teams in the world. Furthermore, morale in the England camp was low. Taylor's reputation had never recovered from the turnip label the *Sun* newspaper had given him after the disaster of the 1992 European Championships. The press had turned against him, and he and the team were the daily targets of scorn and ridicule.

The England–Holland match on 13 October 1993 would later become famous in a TV documentary about Graham Taylor. Every word he spoke on the touch-line, as his hopes turned to anger and finally to despair, was recorded for posterity. 'Do I not like that' would soon become one of Britain's catch-phrases.

The match turned in a 10-minute period midway through the second-half. Until then England had held their own, though they had created few chances. Alan was playing a lone role up front, looking for support from David Platt and Paul Merson in midfield. Both of them were finding it difficult to provide Alan with the ball because the skilful Dutch midfield hogged it, probing for openings. The tireless and unselfish running at last seemed to pay off when he dragged the Dutch defence out of shape to give Platt a free run down the middle. Platt burst through, with only the keeper to beat, but he was dragged down by the Dutch sweeper, Ronnie Koeman.

Another referee, on another day, would have given

a penalty. Even if Koeman had begun his wrestling outside the area, the offence should have been punished with a red card. This referee neither awarded a penalty nor waved the card. Koeman stayed. To add insult to injury, the free-kick from just outside the box was blocked by a Dutch wall that was nowhere near 10 yards back.

In the 62nd minute Holland were awarded a free-kick just outside England's area. Koeman's shot was blocked, but the referee ruled that the wall had been too near and ordered a retake. Koeman didn't blast his second attempt, but floated a sweet little chip over the wall and into the top left-hand corner. The man who shouldn't have been on the pitch had just turned England's task from a difficult one to an impossible one. Six minutes later Dennis Bergkamp sliced through the England defence to make it 2−0, putting the result beyond doubt.

The defeat left England with only the faintest glimmer of light at the end of the tunnel. They would still go through if they thrashed San Marino by seven clear goals, and if Holland lost in Poland. In the event, neither happened. Alan had to pull out of the squad after suffering a slight back-muscle injury and could only watch, as horrified as any fan, when an underhit Stuart Pearce back pass was pounced on, to give San Marino the lead in only nine seconds.

England eventually won 7–1, Ian Wright getting four. But with Holland beating Poland, the result was academic. It was the end, for four years at least, of Alan's dreams of playing in a World Cup. It was also the end of Graham Taylor's reign as England manager, even though there were very few volunteers to replace him.

It was one of Alan's most disappointing moments in football. However, at least there was everything still to be played for with Blackburn. Since the season had started Dalglish had been beefing up his squad. He had trusted Alan's advice in his search for a new goalkeeper and taken his old friend Tim Flowers from Southampton for £2.4 million. Another £2.7 million had gone to Leeds for midfielder David Batty, and just a fraction less to Sheffield Wednesday for the versatile Paul Warhurst.

The team's form became more consistent as Christmas approached. The return after injury of their Scottish centre-back, Colin Hendry, was another important factor in Blackburn's steady improvement, but it was Alan's goals that were pushing them up the table: a hat trick against Leeds in a thrilling 3–3 draw at Elland Road; two more, including a penalty against his old club, Southampton, at Ewood Park; two again, three days later, in a home win over Coventry.

Alan didn't score at Old Trafford on Boxing Day, the first anniversary of the injury. But Blackburn held the champions and runaway Premiership leaders to an exciting 1–1 draw. Kevin Gallacher put Rovers ahead in the first-half and it wasn't until two minutes from time that Paul Ince gave the desperate United fans their Christmas-present equalizer. The draw left Blackburn in third place, just behind Leeds but 14 points adrift of Alex Ferguson's team.

United were looking odds-on favourites to win the Premiership, but Blackburn had shown that they weren't prepared to concede defeat just yet. In fact, they bounced back from the Old Trafford draw with 7 straight wins, Alan scoring 9 of their 12 goals. He had assumed the responsibility of penalty-taking by this time. At Southampton that had always been the job of Le Tissier, whose record from the 12-yard spot was second to none. Alan would quickly develop a similar reputation for cold-eyed nerve and accuracy in this most pressure-laden aspect of the game.

The gap at the top of the table started to narrow. By the end of February it was down to seven points. It was the only prize Blackburn still had to go for because they had been knocked out of both the cup competitions either side of Christmas. United, by contrast, were still on course for a unique treble.

The Premiership became a two-horse race, a battle that grew in intensity as a bitterly cold winter gave way to spring. On 5 March Blackburn made a giant step in the right direction with a 2−0 win over Liverpool at Ewood Park, while United lost for the first time in the season at home, to Chelsea. Their lead shrank to only four points, though they had a game in hand.

The signs of the pressure that Rovers were putting on the Manchester team started to show. Eric Cantona was sent off twice in four days as United were held to successive draws by Swindon and Arsenal. Roy Keane was also facing suspension.

The balance was finely poised when the two teams met at Ewood Park on 2 April. Blackburn were now six points behind, though they had played the same number of games. A win would put them in striking distance, defeat would leave them nine points adrift with only seven games remaining.

The visiting Manchester fans gave Alan the hostile reception he had come to expect. They had never forgiven him for signing for Blackburn. Also, they took as gospel truth those newspaper reports of him turning down United because he wanted more money. The Ewood Park faithful made enough noise to drown out their cries, but they needn't have bothered. Alan was all fired up for the occasion and ready to do all his talking where he preferred it – on the pitch.

Two sensational second-half goals in a 2–0 victory were his answer. The second was a typical solo effort made from nothing but his speed, his strength on the ball and a shot of such force that it would have stung Peter Schmeichel's hands – if the Danish-born goalkeeper could have moved fast enough to block it.

Nine days later Alan scored again, his 30th Premiership goal of the season, in a 1–0 win over Aston Villa that brought Blackburn level on points. They had a marvellous chance to take the lead shortly after, but on the day that United slipped up at Wimbledon, Rovers fell at Alan's old stomping ground, the Dell.

Southampton were by this time in a desperate situation. Branfoot had been fired in January and Alan Ball brought in as manager. Ball had the support of the crowd, something Branfoot had never enjoyed, and he'd got Matt Le Tissier firing on all cylinders again. But Southampton were still leaking goals and losing matches and looking ever more likely to make the drop. That day, at the Dell, though, they got the better of Blackburn and ran out 3–1 winners, with Le Tissier clinching the result with a late penalty.

A week later Rovers dropped two more points

when they were held to a 1–1 draw by QPR after Alan had opened the scoring. At Old Trafford the day before, Eric Cantona had made a storming return from suspension, scoring twice in United's 2–0 win over Manchester City. The results left United two points ahead, but with a game in hand and a superior goal difference. It wasn't a big lead – especially when you remembered that it had been 14 points earlier in the season – but it was enough.

Blackburn were running out of games. When they lost the last but one, to Coventry City, the dream of snatching the Premiership title out of United's grasp was shattered. They had done well to make a race out of what had once appeared to be a walkover, but nothing could disguise the fact that it had been Manchester United's year. The Red Devils had regained their nerve in the run-in, recovering from defeat at the hands of Aston Villa in the Coca-Cola Cup final to win the Premiership for the second time running – and take the FA Cup, too.

Finishing second was an experience that Alan and the rest of the Blackburn team were determined not to let happen again.

CHAPTER SIX

Champions at Last

M ISSING A PENALTY – and at the Dell of all
places – was not the way Alan had planned
to start the 1994/95 season. But then nothing seemed
to be going according to schedule. After aggravating
a back-muscle injury in training, he was laid low by
a virus picked up on a holiday in Portugal.

Alan had to miss the traditional season-opener, the
Charity Shield at Wembley against Double winners
Manchester United. He wasn't the only one. Practically the whole of Blackburn's strike force was on the
treatment table. Mike Newell and Kevin Gallacher
both had long-term injuries, and the club's new £5-
million signing from Norwich, Chris Sutton, was also
recovering from a knock. So it wasn't too surprising
that United won 2–0, with Eric Cantona and Paul
Ince getting the goals.

Alan made a quick recovery from the virus and

just won the battle to be match fit for the start of the Premiership season, against Southampton on 20 August. Sutton was also in the starting line-up, the new half of an £8.3-million strike pairing that the whole of England was dying to see in action.

Southampton had already taken the lead with a Nicky Banger goal when Alan's first-half shot forced a hand ball and a penalty. But he made the classic mistake of changing his mind on the run-up, trying to place the ball rather than blast it in his usual manner. Bruce Grobbelaar went the right way and pulled off a save that had the Southampton fans roaring.

It was a mistake that Alan wouldn't make again throughout the next 9 months and 50-plus games. He made amends for it quickly, too, with a second-half equalizer, bundling in Sutton's header from close range. The new partnership had made a promising start and Alan was off the mark. Three days later they appeared together at Ewood Park for the first time, getting a goal each and combining to set up another for Henning Berg in a 3–1 win over Leicester City. It was the sort of form that would quickly lead to the press calling them the SAS – Shearer and Sutton – the most deadly strike force in the land.

However, it was clear right from the start that they would have plenty of competition for that title. The

Premiership seemed suddenly to be swimming with top strikers – Mark Hughes and Eric Cantona at United, Ian Rush and Robbie Fowler at Liverpool, Jürgen Klinsmann and Teddy Sheringham at Tottenham, Stan Collymore and Bryan Roy at Nottingham Forest, Ian Wright at Arsenal, Andy Cole at Newcastle, Les Ferdinand at QPR . . . The battle for the Golden Boot, awarded to the season's top goal-scorer, looked like being a tough one. And Alan knew that he would have to be at his best to keep his England place in this company.

Since Terry Venables had taken over as England coach, Alan had found himself playing alone up front, at the point of a formation that Venables called 'the Christmas tree'. It meant a lot of hard running, playing generally with his back to the goal, and not much in the way of chances. Sometimes the system seemed to work well. In a friendly against Greece at Wembley back in May, he had scored once in an effortless 5–0 victory. But only David Platt had got on to the score-sheet in the other two games, when England beat Denmark 1–0 and drew goal-less with Norway.

Venables decided to change the system for his fourth game in charge, against the USA on 6 September. He brought in Sheringham to play just behind Alan, leaving Wright and Ferdinand on the bench. The USA were potentially tricky opponents. They had reached the second stage of the World Cup at home back in the summer. Then they had only gone out to a 1–0 defeat at the hands of Brazil, the eventual champions. American teams also had something of a reputation for pulling off embarrassing wins over England.

The game was given an extra little edge for Alan when he read some remarks apparently made by Alexei Lalas, the USA centre-back who had just made a big-money move to Italy after starring in the World Cup. Lalas, it seemed, had never heard of Alan Shearer.

He certainly couldn't have said that afterwards. Alan scored both goals in England's 2–0 victory. The first, an unstoppable right-foot shot, beat the USA keeper at the near post. The second was from a powerful diving header from Graeme Le Saux's cross, after leaving his marker – Lalas – for dead.

Two more goals followed four days later, this time for Blackburn in the Premiership when they kept up their unbeaten run with a 3–0 win over Everton. Alan opened the scoring with what was becoming known as a trademark Shearer goal – controlling a long clearance from Flowers, then turning and powering past the defence before unleasing a ferocious shot. He closed it with a penalty, the first since missing at the Dell. This time he smashed it into the corner, with Neville Southall going the wrong way.

Four goals in four days put Alan in the right frame of mind for the next match, his first European cup-tie. But Blackburn made a terrible start to their UEFA Cup campaign, losing 1–0 at home to Trelleborgs of Sweden. It was one of those days when nothing had gone right and nobody had played well. They looked a much better team two weeks later in the second leg, and in the 83rd minute Alan headed in a corner to give them a 2–1 lead and put them ahead on the away-goals rule. Two minutes later Trelleborgs' Joachim Karlsson broke through to make it 2–2 on the night and knock Blackburn out of Europe.

Alan didn't have much time to dwell on the disappointment. The next month would be one of the busiest of the season – 8 matches in 29 days – and one of the most important, with Blackburn facing their four main rivals for the championship.

October started badly. They lost their unbeaten run in the Premiership, going down 2–1 at Norwich, the victims of a couple of late fluke goals. Next up was Birmingham, for the second leg of a Coca-Cola Cup-tie. They were defending a 2–0 lead from the first leg. It started to look a bit shaky when Birmingham scored, but Sutton made the result safe with an equalizer. It was their third consecutive game without a win and, just to make it worse, the team coach broke down on the way home. As a result, Alan didn't get to bed until 2.45 in the morning.

He was on his travels a few days later, this time to Newcastle for the crucial fixture against the Premiership leaders. Blackburn were forced on to the defensive for much of the time. But they went ahead in the 59th minute when Alan managed to ignore the whistles and jeers of the home crowd to score from the penalty spot. Newcastle then threw everything into attack and, with only two minutes remaining, managed an equalizer. It was actually an own goal, Jason Wilcox's attempted clearance on the line rebounding off Tim Flowers' back.

The night before the game Alan had been able to spend a few hours with his parents, and pop into his old boys' club, Cramlington Juniors. Then, together with Flowers and Le Saux he caught a plane to join the England squad for the game three days later against Romania.

Venables was trying another formation. This time he wanted Ian Wright and Matt Le Tissier to get into the positions to support Alan up front. Romania upset the plan by taking an early lead. Although Alan played an important part in Robert Lee's equalizer, there were few chances to impress. He had a shot cleared off the line in the second-half, by which time

Sheringham had come on in place of Wright, but the game finished 1–1.

Alan's run of five games without a win came to an end on 15 October, when Blackburn fought out a thrilling 3–2 victory over Liverpool at Ewood Park. Sutton, whose team-mates had now given him the nickname 'Trigger' because of his likeness to the *Only Fools and Horses* TV character, scored twice.

Manchester United were the next visitors to Ewood Park for a game that was to end in controversy. Blackburn dominated the first-half, Paul Warhurst firing them ahead with a great long-range goal after only 13 minutes. But on the stroke of half-time the referee awarded a penalty and sent off Henning Berg for a harmless-looking tackle on Lee Sharpe. Cantona beat Flowers from the spot and United were suddenly right back in the game and facing only 10 men.

The furious Blackburn players put up a tough fight, with blond-bombshell defender Colin Hendry even putting them back in front early in the second half. But United were too strong and eventually ran out 4–2 winners. It was a result that only their most die-hard fans could say they deserved, but it moved them ahead of Blackburn to third in the Premiership, behind Newcastle and Nottingham Forest.

With only one win from their last six games and already out of Europe, Blackburn were hardly showing the form that wins trophies. Indeed, some sections of the press were writing them off as championship contenders. But the spirit Dalglish and Harford had created in the team was not one that could be broken so easily. Not for the last time that fantastic season, Blackburn were about to show how they responded to defeat.

The revival started with a 2–0 win over Coventry in the Coca-Cola Cup, with Alan getting both goals. Three days later it was Sutton's turn to knock in a couple, as they turned on the style to beat second-place Nottingham Forest. Two more wins – and two more goals for Alan – and they had put the Premiership campaign back on track within a fortnight.

Next, there was a break from the league action, which the club filled with a friendly trip to Barcelona that went wrong so often that it was almost funny. Flights were delayed. Kitbags went missing. Alan even had his match boots stolen. The only thing that went right was the game, a 3–1 win over the Spanish champions and two more goals for Alan. A satisfying result: only a few days before, Barcelona had thrashed Manchester United 4–0 in the European Champions league.

Alan flew back from Spain on 10 November, more tired than when he had set out, to join the England squad against Nigeria. Both his close friends, Tim Flowers and Neil Ruddock, were in the side that evening. The three were playing together for the first time since their Southampton days. England won 1−0, thanks to a David Platt goal. Alan finished the game on the bench after a nasty knock on the head.

It didn't stop him from lining up to play against Ipswich the following weekend. Nor did it stop him scoring in a 3−1 victory that took Blackburn into second place in the title chase, a point behind the new leaders, Manchester United.

The season had already been marked by scandal, with Bruce Grobbelaar accused of match-fixing, Arsenal manager George Graham accused of taking money he shouldn't have from transfer fees, and Paul Merson admitting to drug abuse, alcoholism and obsessive gambling. But on 27 November all the football headlines were on the back pages of the newspapers for once. Blackburn had gone top after a 4−0 win over QPR, and Alan had got a hat trick.

Sutton had given Blackburn their 1−0 half-time lead, but the second 45 minutes were all Alan's. He made it 2−0 after shrugging off a challenge from Karl Ready that the referee would have given a penalty for − if Alan had given him time to blow the whistle. His second was a penalty, for a foul on Stuart Ripley

by the luckless Ready. And the third was a peach –
one of Alan's all-time favourite goals.

It was almost a repeat of his first for Blackburn,
right down to the man who provided the knock-down
for the shooting chance, Mike Newell. From a range
of around 30 yards, Alan let fly with a right-foot
thunderbolt that crashed off the underside of the bar.

He watched the goals on video at home that night,
pleased for himself, pleased for his friend Mike Newell
who had made an important step in his road to
recovery from injury, and pleased for the club, which
now led the table, one point ahead of Manchester
United.

He was brought down to earth almost immediately
when Blackburn were beaten 3–1 by Liverpool in
the fourth round of the Coca-Cola Cup. For Alan
the game had taken a nasty turn in the second-half,
when he had been brought down by John Scales and
trampled on by Neil Ruddock. Normally the best of
friends, Alan and Neil exchanged some harsh words,
with Alan grabbing his opponent around the throat.
The referee was within his rights to send them both
off. Instead he gave them each a yellow card and a
good talking to. Tempers eventually cooled, although
Alan tossed and turned in bed that night, thinking
over the defeat and the flare-up.

He had plenty on his mind, especially with Lainya

ready to give birth to their second child at any moment. He rushed home from the game against Wimbledon on 4 December, after scoring a tap-in goal to give Blackburn a 3–0 win, and Lainya woke him up at 4.30 a.m. to take her into hospital. It was another girl, a little sister for two-year-old Chloë, whom they named Holly.

Alan felt awful – tired and limp – when Blackburn kicked off at Ewood Park against Southampton a few days later. Mark Atkins gave Rovers the early lead. Alan won a penalty later in the first-half when he was pulled back by Richard Hall. Remembering what had happened the last time he had faced Grobbelaar from the spot, Alan was determined to make no mistake. Going to the Southampton keeper's left, he gave the shot plenty of power. Incredibly, Grobbelaar again went the right way and got his hands to the ball, but it rebounded straight to Alan's feet and he belted it home.

That should have been enough to finish off the Saints, but Le Tissier was having one of his most inspired days and he pulled one back. Then Alan made it 3–1, catching Grobbelaar off his line with a clever chip. Blackburn had secured the three points they needed, but Southampton – or rather Le Tissier – still had the last word. Twelve minutes from time he picked up the ball from the centre circle, dribbled past two Blackburn midfielders, and from 30 yards out cracked a shot that dipped and swerved into the top right-hand corner, past a gobsmacked Tim Flowers.

If Alan had thought his third against QPR was enough to wrap up the goal of the season, he would have to think again.

Blackburn tripped up in their next game, held to a 0–0 draw by struggling Leicester. The mood of the team when they trooped into the dressing-room cheered up when they heard that Manchester United had lost at Old Trafford to Forest. They were still top, now two points clear.

The Premiership was becoming a straight fight between United and Rovers. Newcastle had faded after a sparkling start and the goals seemed to have dried up for Andy Cole. Liverpool and Nottingham Forest had also slipped back during November and December.

They were approaching Christmas. It was always a crucial period in the season, when the games come thick and fast, often in terrible weather, and everyone has at least half a mind on other things. A team that can come through Christmas with good results, and with the players feeling happy about life, is generally a team that will do well in the New Year.

Dalglish allowed a fairly relaxed regime over the

Christmas period, giving the players time off with their families and trusting to their good sense not to eat and drink too much. The players repaid him with a 3–1 win over Manchester City on Boxing Day, and then a 1–0 victory at Crystal Palace on New Year's Eve.

Alan came down with a stomach bug at this time, something he didn't admit to for fear of it being confused for overdoing New Year celebrations. He was feeling well below his best when Blackburn kicked off against West Ham at Ewood Park on 2 January. He perked up when he scored the first goal from a penalty after 14 minutes. West Ham came back into the game and went 2–1 up briefly in the second-half before Le Saux got Blackburn back on terms. Alan made sure of the three points with two more goals – the last also from the spot – to notch up his second Premiership hat trick of the season.

Already knocked out of Europe and the Coca-Cola Cup, Blackburn couldn't have drawn a tougher number for their first appearance in the FA Cup. It was Newcastle away, and the Magpies were keen to get their season back on course after slumping in the league. It was another fast and furious game. Sutton put Blackburn ahead before Robert Lee made the scores level and forced a replay.

Andy Cole had a quiet game for Newcastle that

day, but Alan was as shocked as anyone in football when he heard two days later that Cole had gone to Manchester United in exchange for £6.25 million and the £750,000-valued winger, Keith Gillespie. It was the clearest sign that Keegan was rethinking his plans for Newcastle, and that Alex Ferguson was leaving no stone unturned in his ambition to bring the Premiership trophy back to Old Trafford.

Blackburn kept up the pressure. Despite missing Ripley, Le Saux and team captain Tim Sherwood through injury, they beat Forest 3–0. When United were held to a draw by Newcastle the following day, their lead at the top of the table stretched to five points.

It seemed like an endless succession of important matches. After the Forest win Blackburn were confident of beating Newcastle in the FA Cup replay at Ewood Park. But they lost 2–1, with Tim Flowers making a rare error to let in a late Lee Clark shot. Nobody had the heart to give the big Midlands-born keeper a hard time over it. They all knew that his saves had made the difference between winning and losing many times that year. Even so, they couldn't hide their disappointment. Out of Europe, out of the Coca-Cola Cup and out of the FA Cup. From now on it was the Premiership or nothing.

It looked frighteningly like nothing four days later

when they lost for the second time to Manchester United. It was a hard one for Alan personally. He had a hip injury which needed a pain-killing injection just before kick-off. Needless to say, he was treated to the usual abuse from the Old Trafford fans. He got the ball in the back of the net once, but the referee judged that he had pushed Roy Keane in his jump to head the ball, even though Keane hadn't even thought it worth appealing. All the TV commentators agreed that it was a bad decision, but of course it stood. Blackburn had lost and the balance of the season seemed to have swung decisively towards Alex Ferguson's team.

Three days later Alan sat in front of his TV at home wondering if what he was seeing and hearing could really be true. Eric Cantona, walking off the Selhurst Park pitch after being sent off, had suddenly leapt over the perimeter fence and kicked a spectator who had been yelling insults at him. Alan was shocked. He knew Cantona had a short fuse, but taking abuse from the crowd was part of a footballer's life. He had been on the receiving end of it himself often enough. It was just something you took on the chin, however unpleasant it was.

Blackburn took advantage of United's confusion to record a thumping 4–1 victory over Ipswich, with Alan getting his third hat trick of the season. That pushed their lead back up to four points, with two games in hand. They made a bad start to February by drawing against Leeds and then losing to Spurs.

The Leeds game had been a tough match. In the first six minutes Alan had a shot saved by the keeper's legs, Flowers was sent off for bringing down Brian Deane, and Blackburn were awarded a penalty for a push on Chris Sutton. Alan hammered it past Lukic to notch up his 24th league goal of the season, and Blackburn set about defending a one-goal lead with 10 men for the rest of the match. They almost made it. There were only five minutes to go when Gary McAllister equalized.

It had been their hardest game of the season so far. Several of them were still feeling it in their legs when they travelled to White Hart Lane. Flowers was feeling it in his toe, broken in his challenge on Deane and now keeping him out of the side. Veteran Bobby Mimms took his place. However, even Flowers at his best couldn't have made up for Blackburn's weaknesses that day. The Rovers were no match for a confident Spurs side, and lost 3–1. There were some angry words in the dressing-room afterwards. They'd had a golden opportunity to steal a march on their chief rivals and they'd thrown it away.

With Blackburn's next Premiership game scheduled for a Sunday, United even went to the top of the table for 24 hours. Dalglish's team responded to the defeat with another positive performance, beating Sheffield Wednesday 3–1 in a downpour that soon turned the Ewood Park pitch into a mud-bath.

The playing-surface and weather conditions were little better 10 days later for Wimbledon's visit. It was another day when a winning result had to be ground out with sheer hard work and dogged determination. Alan headed in a third-minute goal to set Blackburn on their way to a well-earned 2–1 victory.

They weren't playing particularly well, but they were still winning. And they had important players now coming back from injury or suspension, including Le Saux, Ripley, Wilcox and Sutton. Their biggest worry was the state of the pitch, which a change in the weather had left bone dry and bumpy. Blackburn's game depended on fast and accurate passing using the full width of the pitch. This was practically impossible with the playing-surface in this state.

The title race swapped around over the next few weeks. Blackburn dropped two points at home to relegation-bound Norwich, but United lost to Everton. Then United put nine past Ipswich – with Cole getting four – to put them ahead on goal difference. On the same day Blackburn produced another gritty, but unexciting, performance to beat Aston Villa 1–0. Dalglish brushed aside questions after the match about United's display. 'You only get three points whether you win 9–0 or 1–0,' he said.

Alan took a bang on the knee in that game and again needed a pain-killing injection before he could take the field on 8 March against Arsenal. It did the trick, temporarily at least. He put Blackburn ahead with a goal in the fourth minute, adding a second-half penalty in a 3–1 win that was harder fought than the score-line suggested.

Alan scored again, a vital 87th-minute equalizer in a 1–1 draw at Coventry. This goal was also his 99th league one. And he didn't leave anyone waiting long for the 100th. Blackburn were trailing to Chelsea at Ewood Park the following Saturday after a third-minute Mark Stein goal. Alan ran on to Le Saux's chip and slammed the ball past Hitchcock. It was a typical Shearer strike – the perfect way to mark his century of league goals.

Sherwood scored later in the half to earn Blackburn another win. When United lost 2–0 to Liverpool the next day, their lead of six points was confirmed. The Premiership title was now tantalizingly close to their grasp.

The knee injury Alan had received in the Aston Villa game still hadn't cleared up, so he was forced to stop playing and training for a few days to give it a rest. This meant that he had to pull out of the

England squad for the game against Uruguay. He had to watch it sitting with his old boss, Lawrie McMenemy, in the stands. Venables tried Sheringham up front, and also gave Andy Cole and Nick Barmby a spell in the second-half, but it ended goal-less.

Alan was back in action for the next Premiership encounter, at Everton on 1 April. Sutton opened the scoring in just 13 seconds. Then Alan made it two in the seventh minute from a cleverly worked free-kick. For the rest of the game Blackburn were pinned back in their own end by a furious assault from Joe Royle's team. The final score was 2–1, with defender Colin Hendry and goalie Tim Flowers as much the team's heroes as the SAS.

Blackburn felt the pressure now as the title grew ever closer. Alan found that he couldn't bear to watch a match on TV that might affect their position. The day after the Everton match he preferred being in the garden, creosoting the fence, rather than in the living-room watching United's game against Leeds. He was delighted to be told afterwards that it ended in a draw.

On 4 April Blackburn won again against Queens Park Rangers. This was another close, tense match, with Sutton getting the only goal. It put them eight points ahead of United, with only six games left.

Their rugged and not always attractive style was attracting some criticism from the media, but it was appreciated and respected by rival teams. On 9 April no fewer than six of the squad – Flowers, Le Saux, Hendry, Sherwood, Sutton and Alan – were named in a Premiership Select side by the Professional Footballers Association. And the PFA's footballer of the year award also went to a Blackburn player – Alan Shearer.

The PFA awards dinner was a terrific night out for Alan. His father and Jack Hixon were there to see him get his trophy, and he allowed himself the luxury of a glass or two of wine. Not even Kenny Dalglish, stealing the best parts of his hastily prepared speech, could spoil Alan's evening.

Then it was back to work. On 15 April Blackburn were held to a draw by Leeds, while Manchester United put four past Leicester City. Two days later United drew against Chelsea, but Rovers fell at home to Manchester City. Ewood Park had been in a mood to celebrate that day, so Alan gave them something to cheer about, with a seventh-minute goal, a first-time shot from a bad clearance. The pitch was water-logged, making the football something of a lottery. Nevertheless, City, fighting against relegation, matched Blackburn's commitment and twice came from behind, eventually to win 3–2.

The run of tough matches was taking its toll on the team in injuries and suspensions. Sherwood and Hendry were missing for the game against Crystal Palace and Dalglish gave the captain's armband to Alan. For once he didn't score in a game where Blackburn battled to another nail-biting narrow victory. Their winner had been scored by Kevin Gallacher, back in the side for the first time in nearly a year after breaking a leg. A few minutes afterwards he was on a stretcher again, after a bad tackle had caused another fracture. His return had lasted only 67 minutes. Five days later Paul Warhurst's season also came to a sudden end when he broke a leg in training.

The chance to grab the Premiership came, and infuriatingly went. Rovers were beaten 2–0 by West Ham, yet another team fighting against the drop, in a match that wasn't for the faint-hearted. Two noses were broken, Hendry suffered a bad cut near an eye, and Alan got a belt in the mouth. The defeat left them still with an eight-point lead, but United had four games left to their two. It was much closer than it looked.

You could see the pressure getting to United by this time, too. Yet they continued to turn the screw, with a 3–2 win over Coventry that cut Blackburn's lead to five points. On 7 May it came down to two when David May, a former Blackburn player, scored the only goal in United's win over Sheffield Wednesday. The match was shown on TV, but again Alan couldn't bear to watch it.

There were just two games left. In a season littered with tough matches, they couldn't have come much harder than these. Blackburn faced Newcastle at home, then Liverpool away. United looked to have it easier, with Southampton at Old Trafford before finishing their year at Upton Park against West Ham.

Ewood Park was packed on 8 May to welcome Kevin Keegan's Newcastle. The fans knew the championship couldn't be won that day, but they wanted to keep the players' spirits up. Alan was reserved for special treatment. Before the kick-off he was presented with the Blackburn fans' player of the year award and the Golden Boot as the Premiership's top scorer. He was a bit surprised by getting the latter because the season still had two games to run, but he had already scored 32 goals, 7 more than Robbie Fowler, his nearest rival.

He made it 33 midway through the first-half, soaring above his marker at the far post to head in Le Saux's cross. The Blackburn fans went crazy with delight and relief. But again, they were forced to sweat for the full 90 minutes. Newcastle took the game to the home team and launched attack after attack, determined to get the goals that would win them a place in Europe the next season. Flowers, though, was equal to every shot and every header, making a series of spectacular saves. His performance that day turned what should have been a 3–1 defeat into a 1–0 victory.

Two days later Manchester United gave a tough display of their own. Denis Irwin's late penalty provided them with a 2–1 win over Southampton. The title battle would go right to the wire.

Although Blackburn were two points ahead, United had the better goal difference. If the Manchester team could beat West Ham – and they were odds-on favourites to do just that – then a draw wouldn't be enough for Rovers. They would lose the title on goal difference. They had to go flat out for a win.

There had been talk beforehand that Liverpool wouldn't make it too difficult for them. They preferred to see the team managed by their former hero, Kenny Dalglish, win the Premiership rather than their bitter nearby rivals. That talk soon proved to be complete rubbish as Liverpool took control of the ball and pushed Blackburn on to the defensive. The game was only a few minutes' old when Sherwood had to clear Nigel Clough's shot off the line.

However, it was Blackburn who struck first, with

Alan racing through the Liverpool defence to power Ripley's low cross into the far corner. They had defended so many early one-goal leads throughout the season, surely they could do it one more time? Ten minutes later a huge roar from the crowd, nearly all of whom were listening on radios to the other game, told them that West Ham had taken the lead against United.

Still it wasn't over. Twenty minutes into the second-half John Barnes equalized for Liverpool. Almost at the same moment Brian McClair pulled one back for United at Upton Park. The fans at Anfield listening to the radio commentary were hearing an agonizing report of ceaseless United attacks and desperate goal-mouth scrambles. On the pitch the Blackburn players gradually became aware that United had drawn level, but they could make no headway against an efficient and free-flowing Liverpool side.

The match seemed to be fizzling out into a draw. They were into injury time when Jamie Redknapp struck a spectacular, swerving free-kick over the wall and into the top corner. Flowers never had a chance of stopping it. The Blackburn players were stunned, unable to believe that their season could end like this. Alan rushed to take the kick-off, but when he knocked it back to Sherwood he saw his captain standing with his arms in the air.

The final whistle had been blown at Upton Park. United had failed to get the goal they needed and which they'd fought for so long and hard. Blackburn had lost to Liverpool. But it didn't matter, they had won the championship!

CHAPTER SEVEN

Europe's Number One

BLACKBURN'S BATTLE to win the Premiership over Manchester United had caught the public's imagination. They were seen as the plucky underdogs who had fought their way to the title, shrugging off each disappointment with another display of courage and 100 per cent commitment. Furthermore, unlike some of their rivals, they had steered well clear of any scandals and controversies. Nobody summed up the professional, no-nonsense attitude at Blackburn during those tense months in the spring better than manager Kenny Dalglish. He didn't say much and he rarely raised his voice, but when he spoke everybody listened, the players most of all.

Dalglish's single-mindedness had held the team together, but at the end of that season he resigned as team manager and took up a new post as the club's director of football. Ray Harford replaced him. On the face of it, it shouldn't have made much difference. Dalglish had always operated at arm's length from the players, leaving Harford with the coaching duties. Although it had been Harford's voice that they had heard most, Dalglish had always been there, suddenly chipping in from the back with a comment that would make them all stop and think. Now he would be there much less often. The players missed him – and it showed. Blackburn made an appalling start to the next season. By the time they recovered something close to their championship-winning form they were out of all the cups and hopelessly way off the title chase.

The only plus point of a miserable year, or so it often seemed, was Alan. If anything, he played better than ever. There were games that season that he would prefer to forget, like the night in Russia when they lost 3–0 to Spartak Moscow and the players turned on each other. There were also moments to treasure.

There were no fewer than five hat tricks for a start. The first two came in a 5–1 win over Coventry and a 7–0 hammering of Nottingham Forest that had appeared to herald a Blackburn revival. They had slumped again after that, but on 30 December Alan scored his 19th of the season so far, and his 100th league goal for Blackburn. It also made him the first player to reach the century since the Premiership had started.

Alan's goals hauled Blackburn out of the relegation zone and into their final place of seventh. He finished the league season with 31 goals. Again he won the Golden Boot and became the first player since the 1930s to score more than 30 goals 3 seasons running in the top division.

What Alan seemed capable of in a Blackburn shirt eluded him whenever he wore England colours. The summer after the championship he'd started in all three games for the Umbro Cup – a four-nation tournament held in England as a dress rehearsal for the following year's European Championships. Attendances were poor and England didn't play particularly well. They narrowly beat Japan, snatched a draw against Sweden and then lost to world champions Brazil. Alan didn't score in any of them.

Stan Collymore, on the move from Forest to Liverpool for £8.5 million, was brought into the team for the Umbro Cup, as Venables juggled his options. Although this spurred him on, the internationals came and went throughout the new season with Alan unable to break his duck.

By 27 March 1996, when England kicked off against Bulgaria, Alan's goal-less streak stretched back 18 months. He was out of the side, too, with a groin injury that would force him to miss the last two matches of the Premiership season. It didn't look too serious, but if it didn't respond to treatment quickly he would also be out of Euro 96. Ferdinand was wearing the England number nine in his place, with Sheringham in his usual supporting role. They worked well together, producing the only goal of the match. Ferdinand was in cracking form, no doubt. Since moving to Newcastle for £6 million in autumn 1995 his name had rarely been off the score-sheet.

A month later Alan was still out of action when England played Croatia at Wembley. This time Robbie Fowler of Liverpool was in the starting line-up alongside Sheringham, but the game ended goal-less.

Alan's groin injury started to improve. On 18 May England met Hungary for their last game at Wembley before Euro 96. Venables put Alan on the bench, and started with Ferdinand and Sheringham. England won 3–0, but all the goals came from midfield. Darren Anderton marked a successful come-back from a serious injury with two of them. Alan was given a few minutes on the park in place of Ferdinand late in the second-half. It would have been the ideal time to score, but the breaks continued to pass him by. At least he was back in the squad for the last stage of the Euro 96 preparations – a two-match tour in the Far East.

The players returned from that tour to a storm of criticism and some difficult-to-answer questions. Why had they travelled so far for two such unimportant games? Why had they played so badly? Why were some of them seen drinking in a Hong Kong night-club at two o'clock in the morning? Who caused the damage to the plane on the flight back home? And for Alan Shearer there was one special question. When was he going to score again?

It was now 21 months and 12 games since Alan had last hit the net in an England shirt. In that time he had scored more than 60 times for Blackburn in the Premiership, but his name stubbornly refused to appear on the score-sheet for the national side. The media were beginning to say out loud what would have been unthinkable a few months before: Alan should be dropped in place of either Ferdinand or Fowler.

Cole and Collymore were clearly out of the picture and it seemed certain now that Venables would play with two up front, one lying a little deeper. Sheringham and Barmby were the candidates for the deeper role, which left Alan, Ferdinand and Fowler fighting for just one place. Fowler was the least experienced, but the same could have been said of Geoff Hurst 30 years earlier. Then nobody could believe that the England manager, Alf Ramsey, would leave out Jimmy Greaves from his World Cup final team. But Hurst, the youngster from West Ham, had come in and gone on to score a hat trick. So it had happened before . . . Alan didn't much care for either the criticisms or the history lessons, and it showed in some of his interviews. He was fed up with all the talking and impatient for the football to begin.

It was a difficult time for all the England players, but Alan was under the spotlight more than most. What kept him going was his confidence in his own ability and the faith shown in him by Venables. As far as the England coach was concerned Alan had always been the first choice for the number nine shirt. Ferdinand was strong, fast and powerful in the air. Fowler was sharp, quick and skilful on the ground. But Alan had the all-round game and, perhaps most importantly, the big-match temperament.

The opening games of most international tournaments are often poor ones. The England–Switzerland match that kicked off Euro 96 at Wembley on 8 June 1996 was no exception. England started as clear favourites, having beaten the Swiss 3–1 in a friendly in 1995, but the team looked tense and anxious. They were working hard, but they couldn't quite hit their stride. Switzerland were making it difficult for them, too, packing the midfield and defending in numbers, but always looking to threaten England with a quick break. Alan, playing up front with Sheringham, was seeing little of the ball and finding himself closely marked when he did receive it.

And then, out of the blue, England were 1–0 up and Alan's goal drought had come to an end. His darting diagonal run into space on the right side of the Swiss penalty area was rewarded by a carefully placed ball from Paul Ince that cut straight through the offside trap. With the ball at his feet and a clear sight of the goal, there was never any doubt what Alan was going to do next, even though Sheringham was perfectly placed for a square pass. His right-foot shot was hit with all the familiar venom and accuracy to leave the Swiss keeper clutching at air. It wasn't the hardest goal Alan had ever scored, but the way he took it proved to everyone watching that he was brimming with confidence.

The goal should have settled England, but strangely it didn't. It was as though the whole team had been waiting for Alan to get one in and, when he did, the rest would be easy. The 76,567 people crammed into Wembley seemed equally sure. The great cry of 'Shee-ra, Shee-ra' rang round the ground long after the goal.

Gradually, though, the crowd grew quieter. The Swiss hadn't given up and England were looking less and less likely to score again. They were losing possession in midfield far too easily and the new Adams–Southgate partnership in the centre of defence was being tested to the limit by the speedy Swiss striker, Turkyilmaz. As the game wore on England were pushed further on to the back foot. Gazza and Steve McManaman were substituted when Venables brought on David Platt and Steve Stone to stiffen up the midfield. Then, with only nine minutes remaining, Switzerland were given a penalty after a shot hit Pearce's arm. Turkyilmaz scored from the spot and the game finished 1–1. It was a tough decision – Pearce clearly hadn't done it intentionally – but the Swiss deserved their equalizer. Throughout the second-half they had looked not only the more skilful side, but the fitter one, too.

If the England players thought they had been harshly treated by the press before the start of Euro 96, it was nothing compared to what was waiting for them after the Swiss game. Most of the newspapers slammed their performance, though Alan was singled out as being free from blame. He had worked tirelessly throughout the match, running and chasing for everything. He had been given one decent chance, and he'd taken it.

The team closed ranks. They knew they hadn't played well, but they also knew they didn't deserve the criticism that in some newspapers had gone completely over the top. It made them a tighter, even more determined group. Their reaction to hearing that their next opponents, Scotland, would be 'more up for it' than they were, was one of controlled anger. England were more than ready for the Scots.

For Alan the game had an extra edge because the man he had to beat in the heart of the Scottish defence was his Blackburn team-mate, Colin Hendry, a player who knew his game inside out. Hendry typified the Scottish team – a little short of flair perhaps, but full of character and courage. Scotland had already held Holland, one of the pre-tournament favourites, to a goal-less draw. Throughout their qualifying campaign they had acquired a reputation for being a difficult team to score against. As England would discover in the first-half, that reputation had been justly earned.

After 45 minutes the teams were still locked at 0–0. Venables had shown what he thought of the newspapers by picking the same players who had started against Switzerland. Yet again they were having trouble breaking out of midfield to make the telling pass around the Scottish penalty area. The Scots had successfully squashed the English attack, but they had created few chances of their own. The game could go either way.

During a snatched half-time interview with Alan

and Venables, TV commentator Bob Wilson suggested that Scotland had probably had the better of the first 45 minutes. 'How many points do you get for possession, Bob?' Alan fired back. It was an answer straight out of the Kenny Dalglish book.

England came out for the second-half with a reorganized formation. Jamie Redknapp of Liverpool was an extra man in midfield, while Southgate moved to left back in place of the substituted Pearce. Almost instantly the English midfield began to get hold of the ball, and to keep it and to use it effectively. In the 53rd minute a quick interchange of passes allowed Gary Neville to get free on the right and hit a wickedly teasing cross from the byline. The ball was there for anyone who wanted it and no one wanted it more than Alan. He charged into the Scottish six-yard box and rose clear above the blue-shirted defenders to crash his header past the stranded Andy Goram. The Wembley crowd, simmering in the glorious June sunshine, boiled over with excitement and relief. Magic-Al had done it again.

Again, though, England failed to kill off their opponents. The Scots gritted their teeth and fought all the harder. And again, England conceded a penalty. This time it was Adams who was punished for a mistimed challenge on Gordon Durie. Gary McAllister, the Scottish skipper and one of the best strikers of a dead ball in the Premiership, stepped forward to take it. Wembley held its breath as he strode up, side-footed smartly to the right and gasped as David Seaman adjusted his dive in mid-air and threw up an elbow to deflect the ball away. Wembley was still buzzing a few seconds later when Gascoigne scorched down the centre of the field to get on the end of Anderton's lobbed ball. He casually flicked it over Hendry's head and then smashed his volley into the Scottish goal. In the space of less than a minute England had gone from the verge of being pulled back to 1–1 to leading 2–0. Gazza, who had borne the brunt of the criticism after the Switzerland game, had taken a leaf from the Alan Shearer book and made his point where it counted – on the pitch.

The victory over Scotland was sweet for Venables and the England players. They had the country behind them, the millions of England fans not just willing them to do well, but believing they could. Now they needed only to draw against Holland to be sure of a place in the quarter-finals. The Dutch clearly weren't at their best. Their squad had been badly hit by injuries to key players and there were arguments in the camp that resulted in one of their players being sent home. Still, they were not to be underestimated. This was no time to be over-confident.

The game against Scotland had been spectacular enough, but what happened at Wembley on the evening of 18 June will live long in people's memories, especially in those lucky enough to have been there. England simply tore Holland apart.

It was the single outstanding performance of Euro 96, and one of England's greatest displays. They took control right from the start, keeping possession and looking dangerous with a crisp, short-passing game, running rings around the mighty Dutch players. In the 23rd minute a late run and a glorious piece of close control by Paul Ince caused the veteran Dutch sweeper Danny Blind to trip him up in the 18-yard box. For the first time England had won a penalty rather than conceded one. Alan had the ball in his hands and on the spot before the referee had finished showing Blind a yellow card. A shot of unstoppable ferocity and inch-perfect accuracy roared past Van der Sar and into the bottom left-hand corner. Alan had his third goal in as many matches, and England had a 1–0 lead.

It was an 11-minute spell in the second-half that destroyed the Dutch. Six minutes after the break, Sheringham thumped a long-range header from a corner into the roof of the Dutch goal. In the England team, Teddy generally played in a supporting role to Shearer, providing the crucial link between the midfield and the number nine, but that goal was a timely reminder of his finishing ability. Six minutes later he provided the last touch but one to what was undoubtedly the best 'team' goal of the tournament. The ball spun from McManaman to Gazza to Sheringham, across and between four flat-footed Dutch defenders, before Teddy's perfectly weighted and directed first-time pass fell smack into Alan's stride 10 yards out from goal. He hit it first time with just the merest fraction of spin off the outside of his foot. The ball was still accelerating, still rising, when it hit the net.

And they weren't finished yet. Sheringham was the first to react to a rebound off the keeper's body from an Anderton shot, to score the fourth five minutes later. England, the team who had been written off as lager-swilling louts a week before, were beating Holland by four clear goals. Alan Shearer, the man who couldn't score for England, had now hit four in three games and was the tournament's top scorer, ahead of the biggest names in European football – Hristo Stoichkov of Bulgaria, Brian Laudrup of Denmark, even Jürgen Klinsmann of Germany. The goal drought had turned into a flood.

As a game the Holland–England match was effectively over. Venables brought off Alan and

Sheringham to give them a rest. England took their foot off their accelerator, and the Dutch managed to get one back in the closing minutes, from Patrick Kluivert. It was a crucial goal for them because, with Scotland winning 1–0 against Switzerland, they would have gone out of the tournament otherwise. Like England, Holland were through to the quarter-finals, but their morale had been so shattered by their defeat that it was no surprise they progressed no further.

In the euphoria that followed England's victory it seemed that the only people who had their feet on the ground were Venables and his players. They knew that just as one bad performance doesn't make a bad team, so one good one doesn't win a championship. Their next opponents would be Spain, who hadn't lost a competitive match since their quarter-final against Italy in the 1994 World Cup.

It was another desperately tight match, with two well-organized defences and confident, experienced goalkeepers snuffing out any chance of a goal bonanza. Neither Alan nor Teddy could find an inch of room and the ball at the same time, while Adams and Southgate were just as in control of the Spanish attack at the other end. The game went into extra time, but the 30 minutes ticked away with never a sniff of the 'golden goal' that would bring it to an end. Almost inevitably it finished up going to a penalty shoot-out.

This was England's first spot-kick duel since that day in Italy six years before when Gazza had cried, Waddle and Pearce had missed, and English hearts had been broken by West Germany. Alan immediately adopted the role taken by Gary Lineker that day, taking on the responsibility for the first penalty and smashing it with not a trace of nerves into the bottom left-hand corner. Hierro stepped up for Spain, but his shot crashed against the crossbar. First blood to England.

Platt was next up, and equally cool, giving even the great Zubizarreta in the Spanish goal no chance. But Amor struck his shot past Seaman to make it 2–1. And then a deadly hush descended over Wembley as England's third champion stepped forward. Stuart Pearce, the 34-year-old left-back they called 'Psycho' at Nottingham Forest came up. He had missed a penalty in that semi-final shoot-out in 1990, but he had volunteered for duty again. Pearce put 1990 behind him for evermore with his trademark left-foot cannonball. Then he turned to the crowd with a gesture that spat defiance, determination and relief in equal measures. From that moment England were sure to win. Belsue made it 3–2 for Spain before Gazza raised the stakes with another coolly taken shot. Then it was Seaman's turn for a slice of the glory as he guessed correctly and saved Nadal's strike. England were through to the semi-final.

It seemed inevitable that England and Germany would meet at some stage of Euro 96. The only shame was that it wasn't the final, because this was a match that deserved that status. It was played at a furious pace between two teams who wanted to win more than they feared losing. It was played in a fine spirit and refereed by an official who knew when yellow cards were best kept in the pocket. It was, in short, a classic.

It couldn't have started better for England and for Alan. In the third minute the team tried a routine Premiership corner-kick, Adams backheading from the near post for Alan to head home from the edge of the six-yard box. It looked so easy. Would England brush aside the Germans the way they had Holland? But just as it had against Switzerland, Alan's early goal seemed to unsettle the English more than their opponents. In the 16th minute, Kuntz, replacing the injured Klinsmann in the German attack, equalized.

There was little to choose between the two sides after that. England had more of the ball but they couldn't make it count and, when the 90 minutes were up, the two sides were still locked at 1–1. Extra time, with the knowledge that one tiny mistake could decide the match, was unbearably tense. Both teams still threw themselves forward, searching for that golden goal. Anderton hit the post, Kuntz had a goal disallowed for pushing, Gazza got his studs to a cross that only needed a fractionally firmer touch to go in. It would be penalties again.

Alan took the first, his third penalty of the tournament. It finished the way of the other two – in the back of the net. But for every successful England strike – as Platt, Pearce (again!), Gascoigne and Sheringham courageously stepped forward – the Germans responded in kind. It went to sudden death, and Gareth Southgate made the lonely walk up the field to face Kopke from 12 yards.

Southgate's shot was saved. The young Aston Villa defender, who had played so well throughout the tournament after only coming into the squad at a very late stage, walked back in tears. Stuart Pearce was the first to reach him. Nobody knew better than him what Southgate was going through. Andy Möller, who would miss the final through suspension, took Germany's sixth penalty. There was nothing Seaman or any other goalkeeper in the world could have done to save his shot. The England dream was over.

Nevertheless, it was defeat with honour. Though Germany went on to beat the Czech Republic in the final, England had come out of Euro 96 as a team to be reckoned with, a team that demanded respect. And Alan had come out of Euro 96 as the most feared striker in Europe, the top scorer with five goals from five matches.

The world was now at his feet. There wasn't a club anywhere who didn't want his name on their team-sheet. But there were few, very few indeed, who would be able to afford him.

CHAPTER EIGHT

The £15-million Man

IF THE SEASON had finished in disappointment
for Alan, the same could also be said of Kevin
Keegan. The Newcastle manager had seen his team's
form and confidence slip in the crucial run-up to the
championship and Manchester United had come
from behind to snatch the title right at the death. In
fact, Keegan was so devastated by Newcastle's failure
to clinch the Premiership that he had offered to resign.
He was persuaded to stay on as manager, although
in January 1997, after a poor run of results, he finally
quit for good.

Keegan had spared no expense in strengthening
his squad, splashing out £6 million to take Les Ferdinand from QPR and another £2.5 million on exciting French winger, David Ginola. Mid-season he
again dipped into the transfer market, buying Alan's
team-mate, David Batty, from Blackburn for £3.75

million, and then making his biggest purchase yet –
£7.5 million for Parma's Colombian striker, Faustino
Asprilla.

But it was Alan he wanted, and when Euro 96 was
finished, he set about getting his man.

Alan's boyhood dream of playing for Newcastle
had never faded. Now, for the first time in his career,
his home-town club had both the resources and the
ambition to satisfy his demanding requirements. Alan
wanted to play for Newcastle, but he also wanted to
win things. After eight years in the professional game
the only trophy he had picked up had been the
Premiership one in 1994/95. He had never been in
an FA or League Cup final, or in a side which
had gone further than the first stage of a European
competition.

It was becoming clear to him that Blackburn were
no longer in a position to satisfy his ambitions. More
importantly, the principal reason he had joined the
club in the first place – Kenny Dalglish – no longer
mattered. Dalglish was about to leave the club, his
new role of director of football having not worked
out either for him or the team.

The question now was not *whether* Alan would leave
Blackburn, but *when* – and for how much. It was a
long time since people had questioned Blackburn's
wisdom in spending £3.3 million on him. Indeed,

that amount now looked laughably small alongside the sums of money that had changed hands with the transfers of Sutton, Cole, Ferdinand and Collymore. If Collymore was worth £8.5 million, then what on earth would it cost to secure Alan's services?

Throughout the rest of June and into July 1996 the rumours flew. He was going to Manchester United for £12 million said one report, later revealed to be a travel agent's hoax. Italy was most of the newspapers' favoured destination, but things were changing. Now the biggest money in the game was in England, and the Italian stars – like Fabrizio Ravanelli and Gianluca Vialli – were beating a path to the Premiership.

The final figure was £15 million, a staggering amount of money for a single player and one that made him the world's most expensive footballer. Yet, if anything, the record transfer fee was less of an issue than it had been four years earlier. Then Blackburn had bought a promising young striker with not much of a goal-scoring record. Now Newcastle were taking on one of the most dangerous attacking players in the world game.

Alan's goal-scoring record spoke for itself. In 138 league appearances for Blackburn he had hit the net 112 times, a ratio of goals to games that no other striker in the top flight could match. But it was more than simply his ability to score goals that appealed to the Newcastle manager. Keegan knew that he was getting a model professional – a player who always kept himself fit, who was never late for training and who was more likely to have an early night at home with his family than be out on the town, drinking with the lads.

He knew also that he was getting a player who would have no trouble with the pressure that would be heaped on him by the fans and the huge transfer fee. Alan thrived on pressure. The bigger the occasion, the better he responded. But this didn't mean that he wasn't prepared to pull his weight on the minor occasions, like the cup-ties against clubs from the lower divisions, played on bleak midwinter evenings.

Alan's enthusiasm for the game and his burning will to succeed had been apparent from an early age. Jack Hixon had spotted them when Alan was only 12 years old. Four years later Dave Merrington had recognized the same qualities. At that stage Alan was a good footballer rather than a great one, but he had never stopped improving.

There's nothing flashy about Alan's game, even though the results are often spectacular. You won't see many cheeky back-heels or mazy, dribbling runs, but then you won't see him giving away the ball unnecessarily either.

The first-touch control, which he worked on so hard under Chris Nicholl and Merrington at Southampton, is now neat and confident. He's become a master – in the style of Dalglish or Mark Hughes – at shielding the ball, holding off one or more defenders with his backside thrust out and his powerful legs planted firmly on the ground.

His strength on the ball with his back towards goal is one of his greatest assets, although it's the surging runs and sledgehammer shooting that invariably bring the crowds to their feet. He's not the fastest striker in the world, but he's exceptionally quick off the mark. Over 20 yards there aren't many defenders, even the fleetest, who fancy their chances against him. And there are few who can match him for power of shot.

Many goalkeepers have testified to the strength of those right-foot thunderbolts (though the left is a pretty nifty weapon, too). It's the accuracy as well as the force that make them so dangerous. Alan says that he prefers to go for power rather than accuracy, but the correct answer is that he generally provides both. Where other strikers wait for the keeper to commit himself and then try to place the ball into the net, Alan will simply hammer it home. He's prepared to hit the ball so hard because he's so confident it will go where he aims it.

Although he's under six foot he scores many goals with his head. Again, this is down to more than just an ability to jump high and use his powerful neck muscles to give the ball a hefty thump. It's about technique and, above all, timing. Nobody hits a moving ball better than Alan, whether he's soaring above defenders to head it home, or unleashing a first-time volley.

The instant snap-shot, when most other players would take a touch or two to get the ball under control first, is another vital strength in Alan's game. He scores so often because he goes for chances that others haven't even seen.

Lawrie McMenemy remembers watching the England–Uruguay match at Wembley with Alan, an occasion when he wasn't in the side because of injury. Every now and again McMenemy became aware of Alan saying quietly under his breath, 'Bang!' McMenemy realized that it was in response to chances Alan had seen for the England strikers to have a crack at goal. The chances went begging.

Of all the top strikers in the English game at present, probably only Arsenal's Ian Wright has the same instinctive feel for a goal. But Wright doesn't have Alan's sureness of first touch, his strength or his ability to keep out of trouble with referees.

Alan's disciplinary record isn't quite up to the

standards of Gary Lineker, who was never even booked, let alone sent off during his long career, but it stacks up pretty well against most of his rivals. Alan Smith, the former Arsenal centre-forward, summed him up simply by describing him as 'one of the few players a manager can afford to just sit back and admire'.

Keegan was soon given the chance to do that as Alan started the 1996/97 season in his customary fashion, scoring goals by the hatful. He quickly struck up a good relationship with Ferdinand (who gave up the number nine shirt for him), and relished the opportunities that were made for him by Newcastle's fast, open, attacking play.

After Euro 96 there was little doubt that England's new coach, Glenn Hoddle, would concentrate his forward play around Alan. In fact, Hoddle went further than that, giving him the captaincy for his first game in charge, a World Cup qualifier against Moldova. Alan rewarded the trust with a goal in a 3–0 victory that set the team off to a good start on the road to the 1998 World Cup in France. A few weeks later, back at Wembley for England for the first time since that semi-final against Germany, he got both goals in a 2–0 win over Poland. Eight goals in his last seven games for England . . .

Alan is still only in his mid 20s. There is plenty of

time left for him to achieve his ambitions. While he may dream of playing in a World Cup or a European final, it's probably true to say that nothing would give him greater satisfaction than winning the championship for his beloved Newcastle.

You wouldn't bet against that happening, especially now that Kenny Dalglish has moved into the manager's chair. It may seem hard to accept, when you consider what he has already achieved, but for Alan Shearer the best is yet to come.

Eric Cantona

by Fergus Kelly

The amazing life story of the Manchester United star player

Born and raised in France, Eric was quickly noticed as a footballer of massive potential. Having fallen out with the French authorities, he continued his career in England, first with Leeds and then with Manchester United. With both he won the Premiership. With Manchester United he won it twice.

Loved by his fans, hated by his enemies – particularly following the terrible night at Selhurst Park – but now acknowledged by all to be a truly unique sportsman, this is the complete story of Eric Cantona's incredible life.

The Ghost Investigator's Handbook

by Marc Gascoigne

'What is the Truth?'

Everyone loves a ghost story – the haunted house on the hill, the mysterious stranger in the night and the dark presence in a bedroom. We all know someone who knows someone who's seen a ghost. But what is the fact behind the fiction? You can make up your own mind with this amazing new book: famous hauntings, poltergeist invasions, fraudsters, hoaxers and men in white sheets.

Look at the evidence, decide for yourself.

The Diary of a Young Girl

by Anne Frank
Edited by Otto H. Frank and Mirjam Pressler
Adapted for younger readers from the Definitive Edition

The Diary of a Young Girl remains the single most poignant true-life story to emerge from the Second World War.

In July 1942 Anne Frank and her family, fleeing the horrors of Nazi occupation, hid in the back of an Amsterdam warehouse. Anne was thirteen when the family went into the Secret Annexe and, over the next two years, she vividly describes in her diary the frustrations of living in such confined quarters, the constant threat of discovery, hunger and tiredness, and, above all, the boredom. Her diary ends abruptly when, in August 1944, she and her family were finally discovered by the Nazis.

READ MORE IN PUFFIN

For children of all ages, Puffin represents quality and variety – the very best in publishing today around the world.

For complete information about books available from Puffin – and Penguin – and how to order them, contact us at the appropriate address below. Please note that for copyright reasons the selection of books varies from country to country.

On the worldwide web: www.puffin.co.uk

In the United Kingdom: Please write to *Dept. EP, Penguin Books Ltd, Bath Road, Harmondsworth, West Drayton, Middlesex UB7 0DA*

In the United States: Please write to *Consumer Sales, Penguin USA, P.O. Box 999, Dept. 17109, Bergenfield, New Jersey 07621-0120.* VISA and MasterCard holders call 1-800-253-6476 to order Penguin titles

In Canada: Please write to *Penguin Books Canada Ltd, 10 Alcorn Avenue, Suite 300, Toronto, Ontario M4V 3B2*

In Australia: Please write to *Penguin Books Australia Ltd, P.O. Box 257, Ringwood, Victoria 3134*

In New Zealand: Please write to *Penguin Books (NZ) Ltd, Private Bag 102902, North Shore Mail Centre, Auckland 10*

In India: Please write to *Penguin Books India Pvt Ltd, 706 Eros Apartments, 56 Nehru Place, New Delhi 110 019*

In the Netherlands: Please write to *Penguin Books Netherlands bv, Postbus 3507, NL-1001 AH Amsterdam*

In Germany: Please write to *Penguin Books Deutschland GmbH, Metzlerstrasse 26, 60594 Frankfurt am Main*

In Spain: Please write to *Penguin Books S. A., Bravo Murillo 19, 1° B, 28015 Madrid*

In Italy: Please write to *Penguin Italia s.r.l., Via Felice Casati 20, I–20124 Milano*

In France: Please write to *Penguin France S. A., 17 rue Lejeune, F–31000 Toulouse*

In Japan: Please write to *Penguin Books Japan, Ishikiribashi Building, 2–5–4, Suido, Bunkyo-ku, Tokyo 112*

In South Africa: Please write to *Longman Penguin Southern Africa (Pty) Ltd, Private Bag X08, Bertsham 2013*